Shelter
from the
Storm
VOLUME 2

RESTING IN THE PROMISES OF GOD
A Daily Devotional

ANDREW & CHRISTY MALONEY

WESTBOW
PRESS®
A DIVISION OF THOMAS NELSON
& ZONDERVAN

This book is a work of non-fiction. Unless otherwise noted, the author
and the publisher make no explicit guarantees as to the accuracy of
the information contained in this book and in some cases, names of
people and places have been altered to protect their privacy.

WestBow Press books may be ordered through booksellers or by contacting:

WestBow Press
A Division of Thomas Nelson & Zondervan
1663 Liberty Drive
Bloomington, IN 47403
www.westbowpress.com
844-714-3454

Unless otherwise noted, scripture taken from the New King James Version®.
Copyright © 1982 by Thomas Nelson. Used by permission. All rights reserved.

Scripture marked (KJV) taken from the King James Version of the Bible.

Scripture marked (NIV) taken from the Holy Bible, NEW INTERNATIONAL
VERSION®, NIV® Copyright © 1973, 1978, 1984, 2011 by Biblica,
Inc.® Used by permission. All rights reserved worldwide.

Scripture quotations marked (NASB) taken from the (NASB®) New American
Standard Bible®, Copyright © 1960, 1971, 1977, 1995, 2020 by The Lockman
Foundation. Used by permission. All rights reserved. www.lockman.org

ISBN: 978-1-6642-7437-2 (sc)
ISBN: 978-1-6642-7436-5 (e)

Print information available on the last page.

WestBow Press rev. date: 08/05/2022

⇨ *Dedication* ⇦

To our rainbow after the storm, Eliana: like your name means, God has truly answered our prayers with you.

"Every good gift and every perfect gift is from above, and comes down from the Father of lights, with whom there is no variation or shadow of turning."

(James 1:17)

To James Maloney, our biggest advocate: this devotional wouldn't exist without your support and encouragement. You are loved and missed.

"…Let us run with endurance the race that is set before us…"

(Hebrews 12:1)

❧ Introduction ❧

*I*f you've read our testimony, *Eight Weeks with No Water,* you're aware of the trials Christy and I faced concerning our son, Christian, and how he almost miscarried not once, but twice, resulting in a two-month hospitalization for my wife. That whole situation was easily the darkest storm we had ever faced to that point. After those traumatic events, conventional wisdom would dictate we should not have any more children. There was inherent risk beyond just pre-term labor. The emergency c-section with Christian's delivery left Christy with some physical issues that, naturally speaking, would not be wise to risk another pregnancy. That we had two sons who were healthy was miraculous enough, and for a long time, we felt to leave well enough alone and just thank God we were able to have them.

And yet, a few years later, Christy felt this push to try for a daughter. When she first broached the idea with me, my response was, "Absolutely not." But over the course of a couple months, I too started feeling a desire that in the natural couldn't be explained. Even still, we knew it would be foolish to rush into another situation that could potentially turn life-threatening to my wife and the unborn baby, so we sought the Lord— not months, but years. Literally hundreds of hours in prayer seeking His wisdom, believing Him for a physical healing that would allow Christy to carry the baby with no complications. We asked Him why we even had this desire to have a daughter when everything in the natural world told us that was impossible. We would try to dismiss this irrational notion, but a few weeks later, here it would pop up again. After a series of supernatural encounters, we finally took a step of faith and conceived.

My wife miscarried at seventeen weeks gestation.

We won't go into the details, but suffice to say, it was a more traumatic experience than the pregnancy with Christian had been, and the end result was a thousand times worse. We had brought Christian home at the end of that trial. We had nothing to show for this tragedy, except ongoing complications.

The pain of that loss, the physical and psychological damage the miscarriage caused, pushed us to writing this devotional. After everything Christy had been through with Christian, surely God wouldn't have permitted *this* to occur. So rather than allow ourselves to get angry and embittered, we sought solace out of the Word, and from those times of healing and restoration, *Shelter from the Storm* was created. It didn't take the circumstances away, but it did carry us through the storm.

More years passed. During the time it took us to research and write the first volume of *Shelter*, we felt that desire to try once again for the daughter we felt God had shown us. Only this time, we faced more obstacles than ever. Surely, we should never put ourselves in this type of situation again! And yet, we couldn't dismiss the words and images we felt God had shown us concerning a daughter. We spent months trying to have God remove this desire that seemed impossible, maybe even foolhardy. But it wouldn't leave, no matter how hard we prayed.

So, we took another step of faith. We conceived, and one month later COVID-19 hit. It would take a whole other book to outline what that was like, a high-risk (in the natural) pregnancy during a global pandemic.

Our daughter, Eliana, was born November 3, 2020, in perfect health. She's amazing, a beautiful ball of energy, nineteen-months-old as we write this, full of life and joy. God had, indeed, answered our prayer: our rainbow after the storm, eight long years after we first prayed!

(Having a newborn is why it took so long to write the second part of this devotional.)

My father, James Maloney, who was our biggest proponent and advocate, encouraging us to write this devotional after the miscarriage, and supporting us unconditionally during the long ordeal of having Eliana, was thrilled to hear we'd finally received the answer to our prayer.

Of course, everyone was isolating due to COVID at the time. But we arranged for Papa and Nana to see little Eliana briefly the day we brought her home. They stayed over by their car, masked up, while we showed them this beautiful baby from under the tree by the side of our house. Mom and Dad were overjoyed, looking forward to getting to know this miraculous, tiny person once the pandemic started to recede. I remember Dad risked reaching out a finger and just quickly touching her teeny foot before darting back to the car.

My mother and father caught COVID in early December. Mom went on to recovery a few weeks later. Dad passed away three days before Christmas.

A year and a half later, we're still devastated, reeling from the loss of not only our father, but the public face of our family's ministry. But even with our grief, we are so grateful he was able to see Eliana once before he went on to glory. Even in the midst of that dark storm, God orchestrated a moment that shined through.

I'm reminded of a statement my dad made: "People think life is about peaks and valleys. One day you're on top, another day you're down in the trough. But that's not true. Life is rarely all ups or all downs. It's a bittersweet mix where in one area of life, you're up on the mountain; and in another area of life, you're just treading water. The only constant in this life is the Lord, that's why it's so important to cling to Him, through the good and the bad, all jumbled together. Only He can carry you through it all."

Amen.

We miss Dad tremendously, though we're not despondent. You can't help but feel your face brighten when Eliana smiles at you. Though there's sadness blended with one of the highest points in our life, we celebrate our daughter, and look forward to that day, long in the future, where we're all reunited once again in the presence of our great Lord and Savior.

In the meantime, we leave you with the second volume of this devotional. We pray it is a blessing and a source of comfort to you, as it has been to us. You're facing mountains and valleys in your own life, no doubt. But we encourage you to find comfort and solace in the Word of God, drawing closer to His Spirit, and trusting Him to provide shelter from the storm!

Andrew & Christy Maloney
July 1, 2022

❧ *Day 183* ❧

"When you pass through the waters, I will be with you; and through the rivers, they shall not overflow you. When you walk through the fire, you shall not be burned, nor shall the flame scorch you."

Isaiah 43:2

Water and fire are often used in the Bible poetically to describe misfortune and catastrophe. Floodwaters overpower and subdue, covering over everything till it is suffocated under its great weight; fire devours and destroys, consuming everything in its path till there is only ash. For some of us, these are pretty apt descriptions of the storms we face during the most difficult periods of our lives. It almost seems as if there will be nothing left at the end.

But this promise from the LORD assures us that is not true: adversity and calamity will not break the child of God. Just as God preserved Noah, a righteous man, He will preserve us from the storms (see Genesis 6-9.) Just as He was with Shadrach, Meshach and Abednego (see Daniel 3), He will ensure the fires of life do not consume us. This is the victory walking with God provides: "I will be with you." If we believe this as a true promise, nothing can overwhelm us! Praise God!

❧ *Day 184* ❧

"When you pass through the waters, I will be with you; and through the rivers, they shall not overflow you. When you walk through the fire, you shall not be burned, nor shall the flame scorch you."

Isaiah 43:2

The word for *waters* (Strong's #H4325) can also speak of "waste" (it's used politely for "making water") and describes "violence, danger and transitory things." It's an apt description of the storms of life that rise up suddenly to attack us and then pass away, seemingly almost as quickly. I believe that's why there's a distinction between *waters* and *rivers*. This verse is promising that even in the midst of the "waste" we face in this life, God is with us; and He makes sure the major floods, as well, do not *overflow* (that is, "drown," Strong's #H7857) us.

Burned (Strong's #H3554) properly means "brand, blister, eat into, hollow out, pierce" (as in a scorpion's sting *burns* into one's flesh.) *Flame* (Strong's #H3852) is different from *fire*, meaning the point of a spear that flashes in the light. *Scorch* can imply being left "dull-hearted, unreceptive, stupid." (Strong's #H1197) This verse also promises that the storms of life will not leave us scalded, hollow and dull because God goes with us through them.

Day 185

"Only be strong and very courageous, that you may observe to do according to all the law which Moses My servant commanded you; do not turn from it to the right hand or to the left, that you may prosper wherever you go."

Joshua 1:7

According to this scripture, one of the components of being "strong and very courageous" stems from observing the commandments that the LORD gives us, walking as He tells us to walk. Most sincere Christians are not carelessly disregarding what the Bible sets forth as God's expectations for His children—we don't live in a state of habitual sin. But all of us from time-to-time "give place to the devil" (Ephesians 4:27) especially when confronted with the pressures and attacks from living in a world system that is opposed to the rulership of Jesus Christ.

"To the right" and "to the left" speaks of *adding* to or *subtracting* from the revealed Word of God. It is dangerous to walk off the well-worn track of godly living as set forth in the Bible, which is the bedrock of God's will for humanity. I admonish you, if you sometimes wander to the right or to the left, get back on track immediately. It is vital for receiving shelter from the storm and being strong and courageous.

❊ *Day 186* ❊

"Only be strong and very courageous, that you may observe to do according to all the law which Moses My servant commanded you; do not turn from it to the right hand or to the left, that you may prosper wherever you go."

Joshua 1:7

*T*he context of this verse is an upcoming battle against the Amalekites, representative of a godless, or atheistic, group: people who had turned to the right or to the left. They represent disregarding the ways of God. Many theologians hold the opinion that the Amalekites were giants. Whether or not this is strictly true, the symbolism presented by the Amalekites is appropriate: the large, powerful godless structure in the world system most certainly makes war against the children of God. Both sides are absolutely opposed to one another.

Of course, the spiritual battle we are talking about here is not a real one as in the Book of Joshua, but there is an analogy that we can make in modern times. While we're not combatting the enemy on the field, we *are* in a spiritual war against a world system that primarily denies the Lordship of Christ. (See Ephesians 6:12.) By keeping on the track set out by the Word, we will prosper wherever we go, living victorious lives.

⋙ Day 187 ⋘

*"In that day it shall be said to Jerusalem: 'Do not fear;
Zion, let not your hands be weak. The LORD your God in your midst,
the Mighty One, will save; He will rejoice over you with gladness, He
will quiet you with His love, He will rejoice over you with singing.'"*

Zephaniah 3:16-17

*D*ay" here represents restoration, when captive Israel
returns to the Promised Land. For us as spiritual Israel,
this "day of restoration" is a lifestyle process, and we can apply
the same principle: be fearless, let not our hands be weak, or
"hang down, be idle." (Strong's #H7503) Natural Israel had
the task of rebuilding Jerusalem, and we also are instructed
to occupy till Christ returns. (Luke 19:13) We are employed
in "rebuilding the temple," a spiritual kingdom within each
of us as we yield to the Spirit's restorative work, which in turn
affects our spheres of influence within our communities, until
the Lord sets up His literal kingdom at the end of this age. To
me, that is what "dominion theology" means—it starts within
us, and we have to work at it.

Keeping occupied is a component of releasing the shelter
we're all looking for against the storms of life. There is certainly
truth in the adage, "Idle hands are the devil's workshop."

❧ *Day 188* ❧

"In that day it shall be said to Jerusalem: 'Do not fear;
Zion, let not your hands be weak. The LORD your God in your midst,
the Mighty One, will save; He will rejoice over you with gladness, He
will quiet you with His love, He will rejoice over you with singing.'"

Zephaniah 3:16-17

*B*ut in order to rebuild the spiritual kingdom in our daily
lives, we must have the LORD in our midst—the Mighty
One to save—it cannot be done in our own strength. It takes a
work of grace on the Spirit's part, with us yielding to that work,
to overcome fear and apathy. *Mighty One* speaks of a champion
Warrior (Strong's #H1368), Someone with the inherent
strength and expertise to complete the task at hand.

The Mighty One rejoices over us with gladness as we work
with His Spirit to overcome fear and weak hands. Our yielding
brings Him glee, merriment. (Strong's #H8057) Working with
Him creates the "quiet" and the "love" that provide shelter from
the storm. It turns our calamities into occasions for "singing"—
literally, a "shout for joy!" (Strong's #H7440) We rejoice with
Him. That word means "to spin in a circle with exultation."
(Strong's #H1523) What an amazing promise!

⋙ *Day 189* ⋘

"Delight yourself also in the LORD, *and He shall give you the desires of your heart."*

Psalm 37:4

*A*lso is connecting this passage to Verses 3 and 5, which admonish the reader to "trust in the LORD, do good, commit your way unto Him, and He will bring it to pass." While it is absolutely true He will "give you the desires of your heart," it is equally true that the conditions of trusting in Him and godly living are components of receiving those desires.

If we find ourselves facing a storm we can't seem to overcome, we need to reflect on our attitudes to make sure we're in line with these conditions. Have we neglected to place the Lord first in our lives in some area? Are we not trusting Him as we should, committing our "way" to Him in a certain area? Are our actions in a particular area not "doing good?"

I do not think constant critical self-examination is a good way to live—if you go looking for problems, you're sure to find them. But we should be teachable and open to the Spirit's direction on occasion to make sure we are truly "delighting" ourselves in the Lord when faced with storms that don't seem to blow out.

✥ Day 190 ✥

"Delight yourself also in the LORD, and He shall give you the desires of your heart."

Psalm 37:4

*D*elight means to "live daintily, softly, delicately." (Strong's #H6026) It speaks of "making merry with" and being "pampered" by the Lord. By seeking Jesus wholeheartedly, with a graceful demure, refined attitude of enjoying Him for all of His perfectness, love, beauty, power and holiness, He will also be delighted to indulge us with all of those good things that subdue the storms of life. *Give* is where we get the name Nathan (Strong's #H5414) and it is translated 174 times as "deliver." *Desires* (Strong's #H4862) is "requests" or "petitions."

When we delight ourselves in the Lord, it *changes* the way we are. We become more and more like Him, and therefore, our desires will begin to reflect His desires, so we will ask of Him only good things, which He is only too happy to grant. Think of it this way, because a child *delights* in making the parents happy, the child does things in line with their requests; and because the child pleases the parents, they are delighted as well to grant whatever is asked, because it is already in line with their will. Shelter from the storm, indeed!

✥ *Day 191* ✥

"For I will restore health to you and heal you of your wounds,' says the Lord…"

Jeremiah 30:17

Restore is translated some 676 times as a variation of "come up" or "go up." (Strong's #H5927) It means "to cause to ascend, to exalt," or "to make superior, to excel." *Health* (Strong's #H724) comes from a root meaning "to make long or drawn out," as when one stretches out tent cords, and is used for "long bandages" that are wrapped around an injury to make it heal up. It means "to make perfect." It isn't just physically, but in every state, being "restored to soundness," every element of life being perfected and prosperous. That's what "restoring health" means.

That's why the end of the verse speaks of Zion as previously being called "an outcast, no one seeks her." God promises to reverse that situation. We could read it as, "I will raise you up and prolong you, perfect you, and make you prosperous in every area of your life." God promises to make our condition in life *desirable* for others—they will see we are well-sheltered from the storms and want to partake of what we have. What a tremendous promise!

❧ *Day 192* ❧

"'For I will restore health to you and heal you of your wounds,' says the Lord…"

Jeremiah 30:17

*H*eal you of your wounds" is such a powerful phrase. Most Christians have probably heard the covenantal name of God, *Jehovah Rapha*, "I AM the LORD who heals you." (Exodus 15:26) *Heal* (Strong's #H7495) most properly means "to mend by stitching" and can be applied to physical recovery, or to restoring a people group, a nation, like in this verse. It can mean "to comfort" and speaks of "pardoning" sins. When we confess our sins, God "heals" our lives by stitching them back together. Forgiveness is a form of healing.

Wounds (Strong's #H4347) is translated "smite, slaughter, plague, stripes, blows" in the Old Testament. It can also be used figuratively—as in being "beaten down" or "plagued" by the storms of life.

As we yield our lives to the Lord in a continuing process, He promises to restore health and heal our wounds. It is of the utmost importance that we are quick to repent and quick to follow the Spirit's guidance—to the extent we do so is to the extent we find shelter from the storms.

❧ *Day 193* ❧

"Every good gift and every perfect gift is from above, and comes down from the Father of lights, with whom there is no variation or shadow of turning."

James 1:17

The context of this verse is James' discourse on trials and temptations. He makes it clear that God only gives good and perfect gifts, and therefore, the negative circumstances we undergo do not originate from Him. It is incorrect theology to believe that God creates the storms of life as a form of punishment. We're not always to blame for our storms, either (though sometimes we are.) This world system, which was originally created without flaw, both good and perfect, has been infected with the principle of sin and death. The vast majority of our storms originate from here.

However, because He is good and perfect, He works within the framework of those storms to bestow His gifts through the covenant we keep with Jesus Christ, executed by the power of His Spirit residing within ours. And further still, this covenant is kept perpetually for all time because the Father has "no variation." He is incapable of changing. So if He has provided shelter from the storm through our relationship with the Son, you can rest assured that will never be altered by Him!

❧ Day 194 ❧

"Every good gift and every perfect gift is from above, and comes down from the Father of lights, with whom there is no variation or shadow of turning."

James 1:17

*G*ood in the Greek, according to Thayer, is akin to "wonder at, think highly of"—something "admirable, excellent or distinguished." It's where we get the name Agatha (Strong's #G18) and speaks of something "pleasant, agreeable, joyful, happy." These are the kinds of gifts God bestows, so if something is *not* this, it isn't a gift from God. *Perfect* (Strong's #G5046) means "of full age, brought to completeness with nothing lacking." So, God's gifts, including His comfort and shelter from the storm, are not partway given. The *gifts* (Strong's #G1394, #1434) James is writing about are two different words: one coming from a root for "credit"—like wages or rewards, a grant; the other from a root meaning "to bestow gratuitously," a bounty. These words speak of "deliverance."

The Father of lights, who has no shadows within Him, gives these gifts of deliverance to His children without any variation. You can rely on Him to always give His best, most perfect, Self to you. No storm could ever smother His light.

❧ Day 195 ❧

*"So I will restore to you the years that the swarming locust has eaten,
the crawling locust, the consuming locust, and the chewing locust, My
great army which I sent among you."*

Joel 2:25

*A*ll these locusts represent a real plague (see Joel 1:4) that
had consumed all the crops of Israel, leaving dearth for
at least more than a year. Mentioning multiple types of locusts
is to show a progression of calamity: they destroyed not only
last year's produce, what had been stored up, but *this* year's
harvest, and what would be used for *next* year's crops, the seed
for the future. Metaphorically for us, locusts speak of storms
of life that attempt to wipe out everything we have worked for,
past, present and future. These locusts are different words in
the Hebrew, representing different species or stages in their
lifecycle. They come from roots meaning: "rapidly swarming;
'licking up' (devouring); ravaging; creeping." (Strong's #H697,
3218, 2625, 1501) So, they represent attacks that creep up and
swarm quickly, devouring and ravaging *everything* they see.

The good news here is the LORD promises to restore what
we have lost, salvaging not only our past, but our present and
future as well! Thank God!

✤ Day 196 ✤

"So I will restore to you the years that the swarming locust has eaten, the crawling locust, the consuming locust, and the chewing locust, My great army which I sent among you."

Joel 2:25

Restoration here is a form of the word *shalom*, which we've discussed before as meaning "peace" (Strong's #H7999) and carries the understanding of a covenant being fulfilled, completed. It's elsewhere translated as "repay, render, reward, recompense, restitution and amends."

When we come into covenant with God—repenting and receiving His forgiveness, keeping His commandments and learning to rely upon His Spirit—we are given reimbursement, compensation, for all the years that the enemy has stolen. Our past failures, our present plights, and our future worries are paid out to us, and we are restored to a lifestyle of peace as God always intended us to have. Your past storms do not have to plague you for years on end—your future is bright in the Lord, and He promises to reimburse your present circumstances with all His goodness because you've chosen Him, and Him alone, to be your shelter from the storm!

❧ *Day 197* ❧

"You shall surely give to him, and your heart should not be grieved when you give to him, because for this thing the LORD your God will bless you in all your works and in all to which you put your hand."

Deuteronomy 15:10

*T*he law of sowing and reaping is a very common theme throughout the Bible. We've all heard it said, "God loves a cheerful giver." (2 Corinthians 9:6-7) And while I believe in tithing to one's local church, giving offerings as we can, we can also be a blessing individually to others. This verse is in the context of giving money to someone in need, but I am convinced the principle of sowing, no matter what you are giving, will yield a harvest at the appropriate time.

This principle is applied to shelter from the storms. Even in the midst of difficulties, keeping a giving attitude, serving others in whatever ways we can, not allowing our hearts to be grieved as we do so, will yield a rich blessing from the Lord. It isn't a magic formula, some plus-minus tally sheet God has, but a law instituted at the creation of the world. (See Galatians 6:7-10.) I encourage you, if you're facing life-storms, find someone to bless, and you will find your own comfort and shelter increase.

❧ *Day 198* ❧

"You shall surely give to him, and your heart should not be grieved when you give to him, because for this thing the LORD your God will bless you in all your works and in all to which you put your hand."

Deuteronomy 15:10

We've mentioned elsewhere that the definition for *give* (Strong's #H5414) is speaking of deliverance, and I believe the deliverance goes both ways: for the one receiving, and the one giving. This word *nathan* is repeated twice for emphasis in this verse to represent, "You shall surely give…" That is, "Give, give!" and don't do it grudgingly. *Grieved* (Strong's #H3415) properly means "to tremble, to be broken up." The attitude with which we give is just as important as the giving itself.

The deliverance—we could say "shelter from the storm" in the context of this book—is manifested as direct blessing from God Himself. "All your works" is all your "undertakings, enterprises, deeds, labors, business, products." (Strong's #H4639) Everything your hand stretches out to will be blessed. The root for that phrase (Strong's #H4916, #3027) speaks of "power" and the place where animals are "set free" to graze, pastureland. An apt image of deliverance if ever there was one! Give, give!

❧ Day 199 ❧

"The name of the LORD is a strong tower; the righteous run to it and are safe."

Proverbs 18:10

N̄ame (Strong's #H8034) in the Hebrew is more than just what someone is called. It is a representation of their very worth, a description of their attributes. That's why so many names in the Bible *reflect* the character of the person so named. It comes from a root meaning "to be placed or set, through the idea of definite and conspicuous position." The word is translated "fame, reputation, renown, glory, memorial, monument."

When referring to the LORD, the word speaks of attributes of Himself that He has chosen to reveal to the world. They are more than just titles He wishes to be called, but components of His very existence. For example, God *is* Love (1 John 4:8), so there *is* love—it exists in this world because He exists. Love is His Name. And since He is incapable of changing His existence one bit (see Malachi 3:6-8), these attributes are unalterable. For a good starting place on the Name of God, read Exodus 34:5-7.

The Name of the LORD is the strongest shelter from the storms of life we could ever hope to find!

❧ Day 200 ❧

"The name of the LORD is a strong tower; the righteous run to it and are safe."

Proverbs 18:10

Strong tower (Strong's #H5797, #4026) speaks of safety due to height; being up high and out of the way of danger, like being in a castle, riding out the storms of life. The roots of the words describe material or physical power, personally, socially, even politically; being "twisted together" with God so that His strength is entwined with ours. That same root is used in the phrase "I will make your name great" in Genesis 12:2. It's even used in Song of Solomon 5:13 to describe a bed piled up high with spices and sweet flowers. This is what the Name of the LORD provides for us.

But again, we should note this isn't automatic. We, being the righteous (that is, those who are in right standing with God based on our relationship with Jesus Christ, having our sins "cleansed," see Daniel 8:14—same word), must *run* to it in order to be safe. We must rush to the Name of the Lord and stand in that power with Him continually. Then we will be *safe* ("exalted, lifted inaccessibly high," Strong's #H7682) above the storms.

✢ Day 201 ✢

"Oh, love the LORD, all you His saints! For the LORD preserves the faithful, and fully repays the proud person. Be of good courage, and He shall strengthen your heart, all you who hope in the LORD."

Psalm 31:23-24

L ove comes from a root meaning "to breathe after" according to Hebrew scholars. To desire or delight in the LORD. Saints are those who are faithful to Him, those who seek Him out and align themselves with His expectations for their lives, those who separate themselves unto the LORD and *breathe* after Him. It is this type of person that can receive shelter from the storms of life by following after their God completely and continuously.

Preserve (Strong's #H5341) means "to keep close, watch over, guard with fidelity, keep secret, blockade." It is the same word used in Exodus 34:7, "keeping mercy." "Fully repays the proud person" can have a positive and negative meaning: those who in their pride seek to harm the faithful will be given their "just deserts" based on God's unfailing righteousness. "Proud" can also have a positive meaning: taking pride in your work, being fully rewarded for *breathing* after God. Whichever way we take the phrase, it means that God watches over you, no matter what you face. Love Him for it!

⊰⊱ *Day 202* ⊰⊱

"Oh, love the LORD, *all you His saints! For the* LORD *preserves the faithful, and fully repays the proud person. Be of good courage, and He shall strengthen your heart, all you who hope in the* LORD.*"*

Psalm 31:23-24

*G*ood courage means "grow stout and strong" (Strong's #H636) and stems from a concept of "fastening upon or seizing" the Lord.

It is an act you take, a decision you make, to strengthen your resolve under hardships to place all your trust solely in God for deliverance, stirring up confidence that He will do as He promises and "strengthen your heart." It doesn't just happen passively with no effort on our parts.

Strengthen (Strong's #H553) speaks of being made "hard, obstinate, bold, brave, solid" against the situations of life. This sounds like an excellent way to live, and it all comes about from our love of Him, rousing ourselves to seize hold of His strength, and ultimately by placing our hope in His trustworthiness that because of Him, we cannot be moved, we will not be shaken, and we will rise victorious through any storm we face. Be of good courage!

✣ *Day 203* ✣

"Blessed be the God and Father of our Lord Jesus Christ, the Father of mercies and God of all comfort, who comforts us in all our tribulation, that we may be able to comfort those who are in any trouble, with the comfort with which we ourselves are comforted by God."

2 Corinthians 1:3-4

There's a lot of "comfort" in this passage. It states that our heavenly Father is the "God of all comfort," meaning the very concept of comfort originates and is sustained by Him. Comfort exists because He exists, and without Him, there is no true, lasting comfort to be found. Because we, as His children, receive His comfort, it enables us to pass that along to others in our words and actions, so godly comfort produces an exponential effect.

The word itself derives from the preposition *para* (Strong's #G3844) and the verb *kaleo.* (Strong's #G2564) *Para* means "besides, nearby"—as in, a *paragraph* are words that are nearby each other. *Kaleo* means "to call by name," and can connote crying out in a loud voice. There can be a sense of urgency and command in the word. "Lord, come stand beside me!" We should bless the Father of mercies that He will comfort us in a time of trial or testing.

༄ Day 204 ༄

"Blessed be the God and Father of our Lord Jesus Christ, the Father of mercies and God of all comfort, who comforts us in all our tribulation, that we may be able to comfort those who are in any trouble, with the comfort with which we ourselves are comforted by God."

2 Corinthians 1:3-4

How the Father comforts us in tribulation is through our Lord Jesus Christ, and through His Spirit dwelling within us. "And I will pray the Father, and He will give you another Helper, that He may abide with you forever…" (John 14:16) You're probably aware that "Helper" in the Greek is *Comforter* (Strong's #G3875), which stems from *parakaleo*: "One called to stand alongside another." The word is used for a "legal counselor;" that is, an attorney or advocate. Someone who would plead your case before a Judge (the Father Himself.)

Based on our right-standing with God, through our faith in the Lord, He has promised to send His very Spirit, the greatest Counselor, to comfort you in times of need. The Spirit will ensure that your rights are upheld before God no matter what storm you face. How comforting! Call upon Him, and He will stand beside you! You can then present that same Spirit to others in need and watch God comfort them as well, as they call upon Him.

✦ Day 205 ✦

"Fear not, for I am with you; be not dismayed, for I am your God. I will strengthen you, yes, I will help you, I will uphold you with My righteous right hand."

Isaiah 41:10

When God tells His people to "fear not," the reason we can obey this command is because "I am with you." In and of our own strength, we cannot help *but* to fear when faced with overwhelming circumstances. Sure, some people can draw up strength reserves and courage within themselves, especially those of strong constitutions—and that's not wrong to have an inner sense of determination—but we must recognize that as finite people, there are limits to our courage; and at certain times, we will all face the emotion called fear, or become dismayed (that means, downcast, disheartened, distressed) because of our situations and environments.

So in those times of great pressure and testing, we need an outside Source on which to draw from. To blend our own human level of strength with a divine, unlimited level of strength. And when we are plugged into that Source, we can then be perfectly capable of obeying the command, "Fear not." Stick close to Him and be fearless!

❧ *Day 206* ❦

"Fear not, for I am with you; be not dismayed, for I am your God. I will strengthen you, yes, I will help you, I will uphold you with My righteous right hand."

Isaiah 41:10

Righteous right hand" is speaking of God's faithfulness in a time of need—it's a Hebrew expression that communicates His dependability to "uphold" His people during the storms. That word (Strong's #H8551) literally means "grasp hold of." Your God will hold on to you and not let go, carrying you through the trials you face. For this reason, and only this reason, can you "fear not" and "be not dismayed" no matter what your circumstances look like.

Dismayed (Strong's #H8159) is another interesting word. It means "to look around" oneself in a state of bewilderment, or to look away and be nonplussed. The idea here is that because God is with you and is upholding you, you have no need to hide your eyes from the troubles you face. There is no need to be afraid and flinch in the face of adversity, no matter what it may be. You have the help of Almighty God flowing through you to stand firm and face your enemies dead-on, knowing you will be maintained and defended through any attack till you emerge completely victorious. What a promise!

❧ *Day 207* ❧

"I will bless the LORD who has given me counsel; my heart also instructs me in the night seasons. I have set the LORD always before me; because He is at my right hand I shall not be moved."

Psalm 16:7-8

*G*odly counsel is one of the greatest blessings and privileges of the Christian's inheritance from the Lord. Many people don't often credit sound guidance or wisdom to be as supernaturally powerful as, say, a healing or a workings of miracles; and yet, to be able to have the mind of Christ (see 1 Corinthians 2:16) is surely one of the greatest gifts He could ever give.

Counsel (Strong's #H3289) not only speaks of God giving advice from His Spirit to your spirit, but can also mean reasoning *together*, devising plans, deliberating *with Him* concerning any puzzle or challenge you might face. That's why your "heart also instructs" in the "night seasons." *Instructs* (Strong's #H3256) carries the concept of allowing your course to be corrected (or chastened, if need be) by your conscience that has been in communication with God through your spirit. Take some time before bed to reason together with the Lord and watch, as you take His counsel, how you rise above the storms of life!

❧ Day 208 ❧

"I will bless the Lord who has given me counsel; my heart also instructs me in the night seasons. I have set the Lord always before me; because He is at my right hand I shall not be moved."

Psalm 16:7-8

Counsel comes when we "set the Lord always before" us. This is more than just a casual acquaintance with Him, but a constant deep, two-way relationship that abides *always*. The idea here is that we recognize *we* are before *Him* always—nothing is hidden from Him. (Hebrews 4:13-15) Since His eyes are always upon us, we desire only to do that which is pleasing in His sight (1 John 3:22) because we know "...the eyes of the Lord run to and fro throughout the whole earth, to show Himself strong on behalf of those whose heart is loyal to Him." (2 Chronicles 16:9) That's what it means to "set the Lord always before" us.

And since He is always before us, that means we are always before Him. He is at our "right hand;" we can reach out and touch Him, that's how close we keep Him to us. "Right hand" speaks of the place of honor, but also to be in a position to defend the person on your left. Peter quoted this passage on the Day of Pentecost (Acts 2:25) to show the Spirit's infilling ties into the promise.

"Cast your burden on the Lord, and He shall sustain you; He shall never permit the righteous to be moved."

Psalm 55:22

The context of this psalm is a betrayal that David faced from someone he considered a friend. It's bad enough facing storms of life from outside sources, but when the storm arises from being wrongly dealt with by a close, personal source, it seems that much worse. I'm sure all of us at one time have felt "hard done by" a friend or loved one. Where this psalm provides shelter from those kinds of storms is in the phrase: "Cast your burden…"

I think many of us have a skewed view on what "cast your burden" means. We often think there is some sort of hyper-spiritual, precise act we have to achieve in order to unload our burdens on God; but in reality, it's a much messier concept. I believe casting our burden means to lay it all out, the untidy emotions, the good, the bad, the ugly, before the Lord and just be honest with how we feel to Him. God understands you are an emotional being, dealing with anger, hurt, pain, and a whole host of "non-spiritual" feelings that most likely aren't very Christlike. You're not hiding anything from Him, so just be honest!

❧ Day 210 ❦

"Cast your burden on the LORD, and He shall sustain you; He shall never permit the righteous to be moved."

Psalm 55:22

Because God knows you are processing some messy feelings in the midst of a storm, so long as you are upfront with Him in working through those emotions, trusting in Him to help you roll those off on Him, this psalm states as a fact: "He shall sustain you." That word (Strong's #H3557) means "to keep in"—that is, "hold you in place." It's elsewhere translated "nourish, feed, contain." It speaks of "measuring" out what is required to meet the need.

This doesn't mean all your problems disappear instantly, but God does promise that as you "cast your burden" upon Him, He will provide the "nourishment" needed to work through that burden. He will never permit the righteous (in this case, meaning "those who trust solely in Him to meet every need") to be moved. That word (Strong's #H4131) means "to be shaken, to totter and slip, to waver, drop, be dislodged or overthrown." Trust and honesty are two great components of casting your burden on Him. Make sure you're giving Him both, and you will not be moved by the storms you face!

❧ Day 211 ❦

"You are my hiding place and my shield; I hope in Your word. Depart from me, you evildoers, for I will keep the commandments of my God!"

Psalm 119:114-115

*H*iding place (Strong's #H5643) comes from a root meaning "clandestine, secret, covered up." It is literally "shelter" from the storm. Think of the Lord as a secret cove in which you anchor your lifeboat till the raging tempest has passed. In the meantime, while hiding out under the shadow of the Almighty (Psalm 91:1), He provides not only a hiding place, but acts as a shield against the buffeting of that storm. We've highlighted elsewhere the meaning of this word for *shield* in the Hebrew: a buckler that is swiftly moved about to fend off a flurry of attacks; the root of the word means "to defend."

The basis for this shelter and defense comes from "hope in Your word." Again, *hope* speaks of "waiting, tarrying, staying." Staying in the Word is the means of staying in the hidden cove of protection. To the level a believer places emphasis on studying the Word of God is directly related to the level of being hidden and defended from the circumstances of life. This is why downplaying the importance of the Bible is a dangerous misstep!

❧ *Day 212* ❧

"You are my hiding place and my shield; I hope in Your word. Depart from me, you evildoers, for I will keep the commandments of my God!"

Psalm 119:114-115

*I*n the context of staying in God's Word to find that hiding place and shield from the storms of life, we could then say that "evildoers" in this passage might refer to those who do the opposite. I am firmly persuaded that to tone down the importance of the Bible can be just as sinful as out-and-out rebellion. That might be a strong statement for those who think, *The Bible is just a nice, old book.* But if we accept by faith the Bible to be the inspired Word of God to mankind, it must take on a much greater import—in fact, it becomes the bedrock for everything we believe spiritually.

Otherwise, how do we know what "commandments" to keep? We pick and choose what is "from God" and what is "from man," and we lose that shelter from the storm. Faith in Jesus does not do away with the Law, it completes it for us. (Matthew 5:17-20) But it is equally true for us when David states: "Your word I have hidden in my heart, that I might not sin against You." (Psalm 119:11) Don't dismiss the importance of hiding in God's Word!

"Remember the word to Your servant, upon which You have caused me to hope. This is my comfort in my affliction, for Your word has given me life."

Psalm 119:49-50

Continuing, then, with our discourse on the importance of living in the Word, we must point out that, according to biblical hermeneutics (how to study the Bible), the Old Testament must be interpreted through the New Testament: Jesus completes the Law for us; God's wrath must be viewed in light of God's love, etc. So much wrong theology stems from improper study of the Bible, and it lessens the shelter we're all seeking.

This devotional is not designed to address every component of biblical study (see *Aletheia Eleutheroo* for an in-depth teaching), but as concerning "shelter from the storm," it's the proper interpretation and application of the Bible that brings "comfort in my affliction." The Word is "health" and "life" to those who are diligent in studying it correctly and taking steps to put its teachings into action. (See Proverbs 4:20-22.) Once we have a firm foundation, we can remind the Lord of His Word to "Your servant" and have cause for hope that He will carry us through any challenge we might face.

≈❧ *Day 214* ❧≈

"Remember the word to Your servant, upon which You have caused me to hope. This is my comfort in my affliction, for Your word has given me life."

Psalm 119:49-50

It is the truth we know that sets us free. (John 8:32) So we're not so much reminding God of His Word, as reminding ourselves of the "word to Your servant"—and it is from that Word that we have cause to hope. "For whatever things were written before were written for our learning, that we through the patience and comfort of the Scriptures might have hope." (Romans 15:4) The Bible is the greatest source of comfort in our afflictions; it creates hope.

The Hebrew word for *comfort* (Strong's #H5165) here is only used twice in the Bible, the other in Job 6:10. It comes from a root meaning "to sigh," and speaks of consolation, contentment. The Bible itself, when studied correctly and in faith, produces shelter from the storm. More than that, it produces "life." That word in the King James is translated "quickened," as in "made me alive." The Hebrew (Strong's #H2421) speaks of "sustaining life" and "reviving from sickness, discouragement, faintness and death." The Bible is a living document (Hebrews 4:12); therefore, it can make *you* alive!

❧ Day 215 ❧

"In my distress I cried to the LORD, and He heard me. Deliver my soul, O LORD, from lying lips and from a deceitful tongue."

Psalm 120:1-2

Psalm 120 is called a "song of degrees" (Verse 1, Strong's #H4609) which refers to "thoughts that arise" or a "climactic progression." The word means "stairsteps," to go up higher. David is using this song to lament being a sojourner in a land that is "for war" when he is "for peace." (Verse 7) This is an appropriate picture of our lives in this world—we want to seek peace, but the circumstances (and often people) arrayed against us want to seek war. These circumstances come against us in varying degrees, building up until they seem to threaten overwhelming us.

David's response to these building circumstances is the correct one: he sought the LORD in prayer with an expectation in hope that He would deliver his soul from the attacks he was under. From time to time, we will all face mounting pressures, even if we're seeking only peace, because we are dwelling in a world system that is influenced by the father of lies (John 8:44), but as we cry out to God, we can expect to find His deliverance.

✥ *Day 216* ✥

"In my distress I cried to the LORD, and He heard me. Deliver my soul, O LORD, from lying lips and from a deceitful tongue."

Psalm 120:1-2

*D*istress (Strong's #H6869) is a feminine form of a noun coming from a root that means "an adversary, an enemy, a rival, one who vexes." It can speak of an actual entity (a real person, or the devil) and also situations or conditions that are distressing. It is rendered as "tightness, adversity, anguish, trouble, straits" and is the word for a "hard pebble or flint"—something hard and irritating you don't want stuck in the bottom of your shoe. Metaphorically, these are the storms of life.

As this passage points out, "lying lips" and "a deceitful tongue" are instigators of these storms. Your adversary or rival's slanderous, falsehearted words—coming either from the devil or a person in your life—are what David called "sharp arrows" or "coals of juniper." (Verse 4) The juniper bush, according to Gesenius, has a bitter root that the poor were accustomed to eating. In other words, the attacks are bitter, hot words your enemy is trying to get you to swallow. The good news is: crying out to the LORD in faith, He will hear you and deliver your soul!

✎ Day 217 ✎

"Therefore comfort each other and edify one another, just as you also are doing."

1 Thessalonians 5:11

*P*aul's instruction in this verse to comfort and edify one another is in light of the previous passage, outlining the distinction between "children of the day" and "children of the night." He makes it clear that the "children of light" are not appointed to God's wrath, but to salvation through our faith in Jesus Christ. (Verse 9) This doesn't mean we have no tribulation or difficulty—it does not entirely exclude us from the storms of life; but in Verse 10, Paul goes on to say, "whether we wake or sleep," we'll live with Christ. And therefore, because of that truth, we should comfort and edify one another as brethren in Him.

Take comfort in the truth that you are a child of the light. Yes, be sober-minded, paying attention to what's going on around you so you can avoid as many hardships as possible; continue to walk in love and faith, believing in the hope of salvation through the storms. (Verse 8) But realize that God has selected you for salvation (rescue) through it all because of your relationship with Jesus Christ.

✥ *Day 218* ✥

"Therefore comfort each other and edify one another, just as you also are doing."

1 Thessalonians 5:11

*C*omfort means to "encourage" one another. It's the same Greek word used to describe the work of the Holy Spirit in the Christian's life. (Strong's #G3870) It means "to call alongside, to summon." It carries a connotation of command. (See 1 Thessalonians 4:18.) This shows me we are instructed to take the comfort we have received from God's Spirit and comfort others with it. (2 Corinthians 1:3-4) By doing so, we ensure a fresh, never-ending flow of comfort and encouragement from God, to us, and out to others through us—the very definition of shelter from the storm, as I see it.

Edify (Strong's #G3619) means to "build up." In the Greek, it's a compound word made up of "house(hold)," implying a family and their home, and "housetop"—those Middle Eastern homes with flat roofs where the family gathers to walk, meditate and pray. The idea to convey here is we are admonished to encourage and build one another up like a family. As we do so we increase the comfort and edification we're all seeking as shelter from the storms we face. Let's make sure we're doing this, just as the Thessalonians were also doing!

❧ *Day 219* ❧

"I will lift up my eyes to the hills—from whence comes my help? My help comes from the LORD, who made heaven and earth."

Psalm 121:1-2

L ift up my eyes" is a reference to prayer, but there is also an expectation for that prayer to be answered. It's not just asking, but asking in faith, expecting to be answered. Looking and anticipating for that help to come. When Jesus raised Lazarus from the dead, notice He "looked up," but His prayer wasn't in an oh, please, please, please fashion. Rather, He was just audibly stating a fact He already knew: "Father, I thank You that You have heard Me. And I know that You always hear Me, but because of the people who are standing by I said this, that they may believe that You sent Me." (John 11:41-42) Then He commanded Lazarus to come forth.

When we are seeking the Lord's intervention in the midst of a storm, we too must "lift up" our eyes, but let's also duplicate Jesus' expectation that the Father has *already* heard our prayer for help. It's okay to ask for help, certainly, but double-check your heart attitude to ensure you're *expecting* the answer to come. Those kinds of prayers are sure to bring shelter from the storm!

❧ *Day 220* ❧

"I will lift up my eyes to the hills—from whence comes my help? My help comes from the Lord, who made heaven and earth."

Psalm 121:1-2

*T*o the hills" can be read two ways, both of which are appropriate interpretations when seeking shelter from the storm. One way is to read the sentence as a question: "Shall I look to the hills for my help?" In pagan religions, hilltops are often "sacred" places where idols are worshipped. (See 1 Kings 14:23.) So the psalmist is asking, "Shall I look to them for my help?" The question is rhetorical, as the answer is obviously, "No." We must also be convinced of this. Our shelter comes from no other Source than God alone.

The second interpretation is that "hills" refers to the hills of Moriah and Mount Zion where the ark of God's covenant was kept. I like this interpretation perhaps better. Our expectation (lifting up our eyes) beyond the "high places" of man's own machinations, beyond the false security of "idolatry," to the source of God's covenant with us—that is, the Lord Jesus Christ. Our help comes from Him, who made heaven and earth. Our Shelter is above it all—set your eyes on Him!

❧ *Day 221* ❧

"Love suffers long and is kind; love does not envy; love does not parade itself, is not puffed up; does not behave rudely, does not seek its own, is not provoked, thinks no evil; does not rejoice in iniquity, but rejoices in the truth; bears all things, believes all things, hopes all things, endures all things. Love never fails."

1 Corinthians 13:4-8

This is the famous "Divine Love" chapter, a follow up to the spiritual gifts outlined in Chapter 12 (the so-called "Divine Power" chapter), continuing into Chapter 14, the "Divine Energy" chapter. The purpose of this three-act structure is to show that the God-kind of love, *agape* (Strong's #G26), is the only true motivation factor in pursuing spiritual gifts and prophecy/tongues. *Agape* is speaking about the kind of love that shows benevolence to another, which is why the KJV translates it as "charity."

Paul is saying, then, you may be the most anointed person on the planet, seeing all kinds of signs and wonders; or the most powerful worshipper with prophetic utterance, speaking in tongues—but if love isn't the motivating factor, it's all "sounding brass." (Verse 1) Therefore, shelter from our own storms comes from operating in charitable love. Do everything from a stance of love!

"Love suffers long and is kind; love does not envy; love does not parade itself, is not puffed up; does not behave rudely, does not seek its own, is not provoked, thinks no evil; does not rejoice in iniquity, but rejoices in the truth; bears all things, believes all things, hopes all things, endures all things. Love never fails."

1 Corinthians 13:4-8

So if we're seeking shelter from our own trials and difficulties, and we know that one of the major keys to unlocking that shelter comes from operating in charitable love, we need to make sure we understand how that love operates, right? Makes sense.

It isn't such a difficult concept to grasp, but it *can* be difficult to walk in love on a daily basis. And yet, Paul tells us it's the true pursuit of a love-walk that unlocks the power of spiritual gifts, prophecy and tongues. Even our heavenly prayer language is made effective through love.

What is love, then? Just as the above passage states, it's longsuffering, even when people are difficult to deal with; it's kind, not envious, not exploitative or prideful, isn't rude, self-seeking, easily provoked, or evil-thinking. It loves the truth and despises sin. It bears, believes, hopes, endures *all things*. It never fails. So the question to consider today is: How's your love-walk?

❧ Day 223 ❦

"The LORD is my strength and song, and He has become my salvation; He is my God, and I will praise Him; my father's God, and I will exalt Him."

Exodus 15:2

*T*he context of this passage is God's miraculous deliverance of the children of Israel at the Red Sea. Moses and the Israelites burst into this celebratory song that declares God is their "strength and song." The root for *strength* (Strong's #H5797) speaks of "hardening, to make secure." *Song* means "the object of my praise." (Strong's #H2176) When we recognize this key: He makes us strong through our praise, we are in a position for Him to become our salvation.

The phrasing "become my salvation" (Strong's #H3444) is interesting in the Hebrew. It is the word used for Yeshua (Jesus) placed in what's called "passive participle," which is a verb that can function as a noun. What this means for us is He's not just able to save us as an act—He *is* the Salvation. When we praise Him, He doesn't just save us from the storms as an action He can do—He is Salvation in and of Himself. So we're not seeking something He can do, but rather something that He is. We're simply seeking more of Him!

❧ *Day 224* ❦

"The Lᴏʀᴅ is my strength and song, and He has become my salvation; He is my God, and I will praise Him; my father's God, and I will exalt Him."

Exodus 15:2

*P*art of the salvation that He is comes from our declaration that He is our God. And of course, what else do you do with God but praise Him? That word for *praise* actually can be rendered "keep at home" or "prepare a habitation" for Him—literally to "sit down and rest with Him." (Strong's #H5115) Since we declare He is our God, we will abide, dwell, with Him, and He will become our Salvation.

Exalt (Strong's #H7311) means "to lift up" or to "hold up high." When we magnify the Lord above our problems, He becomes the Salvation from the difficult circumstances we are facing. To the level we "sit down and rest" with Him is the level to which He is raised up above our difficulties and becomes the Salvation we are seeking. Remember, you're not so much seeking Him to bail you out of problems as to be raised up higher than those problems (through praise and exaltation), and reflexively, because He is Salvation—you will be saved from your storms!

"For God has not given us a spirit of fear, but of power and of love and of a sound mind."

2 Timothy 1:7

*I*n the Greek, there are different words for *not*. The one used here (Strong's #G3756) means "absolutely negative." In English, we might say "cannot"—completely impossible under any circumstances. Compare to the other word for *not* (Strong's #G3361) which means "no, unless…" implying you have a choice to make which *could* change "no" to "yes."

So Paul is telling Timothy here that it is an absolute impossibility for God to give us a "spirit of fear." This means that if we have fear about our circumstances, it is not (completely, wholly, unconditionally *not*) from God, no exceptions.

This word for *fear* (Strong's #G1167) is unique in the whole New Testament to just this one verse. Normally, the word for *fear* is where we would get the English word "phobia," but in this special case, the word comes from a root for "dread" and means "cowardice, timidity." So all this means to say, when facing the struggles of life, none of the dread, anxiety, hesitation, weakness, or apprehension comes from God—we should reject it as an absolute negative, completely! God has not given it to us.

☙ *Day 226* ❧

"For God has not given us a spirit of fear, but of power and of love and of a sound mind."

2 Timothy 1:7

*I*f God has *not* given us a spirit of fear—what has He given us a spirit of, then?

Power (Strong's #G1411) is "inherent strength, ability," and I'm sure most of you know is where we get English words like *dynamo* and *dynamite*. It especially refers to miraculous power, the miracle itself, and is translated "wondrous or mighty works" in the Bible. It's the word for *virtue* in Mark 5:30. The power of the Spirit is resident within your spirit.

Love (Strong's #G26) speaks of "affection, goodwill, benevolence"—that is, a charitable spirit which desires to share that miraculous power with your fellow brethren.

Sound mind (Strong's #G4995) comes from a root meaning "sober, temperate" and speaks of moderation, discipline, self-control, in all our dealings.

These three attributes *are* given to your spirit-man to enable you through the release of the miraculous, with brotherly love and charity, and through a restrained, even-keeled disposition in your mind, will and emotions, to overcome any storms you might face!

❧ *Day 227* ❧

"…Do not let your heart faint, do not be afraid, and do not tremble or be terrified because of them; for the LORD your God is He who goes with you, to fight for you against your enemies, to save you."

Deuteronomy 20:3-4

The context for this declaration is the guidelines the Israelites were to follow when going to battle against an enemy. The priests were to make this proclamation just prior to the engagement in order to remind Israel they did not fight on their own, but rather, that God fought alongside them against their enemies. Why the Israelites could be assured that God Himself was going with them into battles was based upon the covenant He had made with them. When they kept their end of the covenant, they were assured victory no matter what enemy they faced.

We have an even better covenant than they did, because our new covenant is ratified by Christ's blood. (See Hebrews 8.) In this current age, most of us do not go into battle with another nation—but we do wage war against the storms of life that are brewed up by the corrupted world system we live in. We do have "enemies" that come against us, and the admonishment for the Israelites applies to us today. Do not be afraid—God goes with you!

❦ *Day 228* ❦

*"...Do not let your heart faint, do not be afraid, and do not tremble or be terrified because of them; for the L*ORD *your God is He who goes with you, to fight for you against your enemies, to save you."*

Deuteronomy 20:3-4

*T*he Hebrew word for *enemies* (Strong's #H341) comes from the verb "to hate," and Gesenius likens the word to the idea of "blowing, puffing" against us in anger and hatred. Our "enemies" today huff and puff against us in rage—an apt image for the storms of life, indeed. They seek to blow us down, run roughshod right over us, so that we cannot rise against them.

We are not to be *faint* in the face of stormy circumstances. That word (Strong's #H7401) means "mollified, tender, weak, soft, timid." In the face of trials, we're not to be complacent and apathetic. Rather, we're to rise up against them, knowing that our God fights alongside with us, to save us from those stormy enemies.

If we truly believed that God walked alongside us into battle, we would be utterly fearless in the face of adversity. "Fight for you" (Strong's #H3898) is a poetic phrase that means "to eat, devour" your enemies. God walks with you to destroy, consume, the storms you face!

46

✑ Day 229 ✑

"Whom have I in heaven but You? And there is none upon earth that I desire besides You. My flesh and my heart fail; but God is the strength of my heart and my portion forever."

Psalm 73:25-26

We have no other Advocate above us other than our God. Looking to any other celestial source for strength is wasted energy—there is nothing else "out there" for us except the LORD. People spend lifetimes in frustration looking for the higher way, the path above the stormy lives we lead down here on earth. But that pursuit of false comfort, apart from a vivid, brilliant relationship with the living God, is just another storm, in and of itself—one with dire consequences that last for eternity. Of all the decisions you make, choosing to pursue the true God is the most important. Everything falls into place once that decision is made. Note, I didn't say everything becomes "easy"—but it *will* work out to your good ultimately. On the other side, there is nothing on earth to *desire* but Him. That word (Strong's #H2654) means to "bend or curve," and metaphorically means to incline toward something. There is nothing on this planet or in the universe more worthwhile to bend our time and energy toward than our relationship with God!

❦ Day 230 ❦

"Whom have I in heaven but You? And there is none upon earth that I desire besides You. My flesh and my heart fail; but God is the strength of my heart and my portion forever."

Psalm 73:25-26

*M*y flesh and my heart" speaks of our entire existence. Our bodies and our souls are not strong enough to overcome the storms of life. If we rely only upon our own meager existence, we would *fail* utterly. That word (Strong's #H3615) means "to be finished, to cease, to be consumed." Without God, we're "done for" in the most complete sense of the phrase. See how important it is to desire God above all else?

Strength (Strong's #H6697) is the word for "rock" and stems from a root for "compress together"—the idea that a rock is matter squeezed together tightly, densely; and from being compacted together with God, our strength is increased. We must squash ourselves together with God so compactly, so closely, that His strength becomes our strength. *Portion* (Strong's #H2506) speaks of smooth stones that were used for dividing lots in an inheritance, further reinforcing the "God is our Rock" notion. Squeeze yourself together with the Rock!

❧ Day 231 ❧

"'And you shall love the LORD your God with all your heart, with all your soul, with all your mind, and with all your strength.' This is the first commandment. And the second, like it, is this: 'You shall love your neighbor as yourself.' There is no other commandment greater than these."

Mark 12:30-31

I love the Lord's response to the scribe after he agreed with Him that these were the two foremost commandments, "more than all the whole burnt offerings and sacrifices." (Verse 33) Jesus saw the man answered wisely and told him, "You are not far from the kingdom of God." (Verse 34) After that, no one "dared question Him."

Jesus expands the great commandment of Deuteronomy 6:4 to include the phrase "with all your mind" to encompass the entirety of a person's existence: their mind, will, emotions, spirit and body. In other words, complete surrender. There isn't a "halfway" with God—all of you gets all of Him. We know that the kingdom of God represents the perfection of everything we could ever seek. By loving Him wholly, it puts us in proximity to that kingdom, and therefore, in a position to receive everything we need in the name of shelter from the storm.

❧ *Day 232* ☙

"'And you shall love the LORD your God with all your heart, with all your soul, with all your mind, and with all your strength.' This is the first commandment. And the second, like it, is this: 'You shall love your neighbor as yourself.' There is no other commandment greater than these."

Mark 12:30-31

According to 1 John 4:8, "God is love." This means it is more than just an emotion God possesses—it is a component of His makeup, His substance. The concept of love exists because He exists. It isn't something He can do; it is something that *He is.* This is why the prime commandment is so important. We are commanded to love Him simply for who He is, not only for what He does. This is a primary component to finding shelter from the storms: love God, no matter what. It's in line with the admonition: "But seek first the kingdom of God and His righteousness, and all these things shall be added to you." (Matthew 6:33) God extends this commandment to include our fellow man. To love your neighbor (that is, one "nearby" you, Strong's #G4139; anyone you come in contact with—not just the people you like) as you love yourself means to treat them as you want to be treated. The Golden Rule is a condition of shelter from the storm!

❧ Day 233 ❧

"A man's heart plans his way, but the LORD directs his steps."

Proverbs 16:9

*T*he word for *way* (Strong's #H1870) comes from a root meaning "to tread or bend." It was used to describe an archer stringing a bow, because one "treads" on the bow to bend it, and came to mean the way a person walked, physically or metaphorically: the course of one's life, the manner and habits in which one "walks" through the world.

This passage states that we ourselves plan the "way" we walk—we "string our own bows," so to speak. And that's not a bad thing. As rational, free-thinking people, God has given us the ability to choose our own path, for good or bad, and we can use our "bow" for defense or offense.

It is not wrong to plan our own way. Each of us must make dozens, perhaps hundreds, of decisions on a daily basis, and some of them can have lasting impact on the "way we walk" for the rest of our lives. It is important, then, that our decisions are carefully weighed to avoid as many rough patches in the course of our lives as we can.

❧ *Day 234* ☙

"A man's heart plans his way, but the LORD directs his steps."

Proverbs 16:9

*B*ut it is more than just us being careful to pick our "way" through life, as if there is no outside involvement whatsoever. There is an element of faith involved that God is orchestrating our steps. Again, this is not a bad thing. We *want* God to create our paths, because we know His way is best. That's not to say God has created robots, moving through life on rote, executing some program. Rather, He has incorporated our plans, our hearts' desires (Psalm 37:4), into His own.

As we submit our paths unto Him (Proverbs 3:5-6), trusting in Him with all our heart, soul, mind and strength (Deuteronomy 6:4), we can be assured by faith that He is directing our steps, even when the pathway seems difficult and full of stormy situations.

The Hebrew for *directs* (Strong's #H3559) means "to establish or prepare, to make ready." God is in the unique position, outside the constraints of linear time, knowing the end from the beginning (Isaiah 46:10), to prepare the steps of those who love Him and are called according to His purpose. (Romans 8:28) Take comfort in knowing this truth!

ꙮ Day 235 ꙮ

"But the Lord is faithful, who will establish you and guard you from the evil one. And we have confidence in the Lord concerning you, both that you do and will do the things we command you."

2 Thessalonians 3:3-4

Paul is showing a distinction here between "all men have not faith" (Verse 2) and Jesus who is "faithful." If you've been living in this world for any length of time, there is no doubt that you have discovered every human being, even those closest to you, in your immediate family, are capable of "having no faith." The word *faithful* means "trustworthy, reliable, steadfast, consistent, dependable." Sweeping from one end to the other, humanity, down to a person, is plagued by shortcomings when it comes to being faithful.

However, Jesus Christ is entirely faithful. The perfect indwelling of fully God and fully Man in one Body, He is the epitome of faithful perfection. He will never leave you nor forsake you. (Deuteronomy 31:6) Jesus cannot ever "drop the ball." By putting our trust in Him, receiving His indwelling Spirit into our own, we are put on a path of becoming more faithful throughout the course of our lives—but thankfully, Jesus is already faultless! He will guard you perfectly.

❧ *Day 236* ❧

"But the Lord is faithful, who will establish you and guard you from the evil one. And we have confidence in the Lord concerning you, both that you do and will do the things we command you."

2 Thessalonians 3:3-4

Since Jesus is impeccably flawless in His faithfulness, we can be assured that He will "establish" and "guard" us through any storm. The Greek for *establish* (Strong's #G4741) is most likely derived from a word meaning "to stand still." It speaks of being "rendered constant" (that is, made "faithful" as Jesus is) and "strengthened, firmly stable." Steadfastly set in a fixed condition, resolute. This word pertains to your dealings with God—He will turn you into someone faithful, as He is faithful. (That's why Paul says he's confident the Thessalonians do and will continue to do the things he commands them in the Lord. Not because of *their* inherent steadfastness, but because of His.)

Secondly, Jesus will "guard you from the evil one." *Guard* (Strong's #G5442) stems from a root for a "tribe or clan" kept isolated from another one. So here it means Jesus takes great care to watch over you to keep you separated from evil, providing shelter from the storms.

"But without faith it is impossible to please Him, for he who comes to God must believe that He is, and that He is a rewarder of those who diligently seek Him."

Hebrews 11:6

Impossible (Strong's #G102) has its root in the word *dynamis*, which most of you probably recognize as "power" or "ability." In this passage, the word means "no power" or "weak," implying an inability to perform a task (pleasing Him.) So that means faith gives ability or power to unlock the "rewards" of seeking Him.

Now, faith is often presented as some lofty theological concept, some intangible force we have to have a certain amount of in order to get God to reward us: "If I *just* had enough faith, I could get God to heal me." Sometimes, the concept of faith is used to put a whammy on people.

But the word itself (Strong's #G4102) is a very simple concept: "a conviction, persuasion, confidence," something you sincerely believe. Being firmly persuaded in something. Faith is energized by God to bring about the desired result—we're not convincing Him to do *anything*. Take note of Mark 9:23-25 for the next entry.

❧ Day 238 ❧

"But without faith it is impossible to please Him, for he who comes to God must believe that He is, and that He is a rewarder of those who diligently seek Him."

Hebrews 11:6

Jesus requires faith; yes, that is certainly true. (Mark 9:23) But He will "help our unbelief" (Verse 24) by rewarding those who diligently seek Him. That's faith in action. Faith starts with belief that "He is." In other words, to truly believe that God exists: moving beyond doubting whether or not He's real. You have to settle this in your heart before you do anything else with Him. There is no way to acceptably please Him if we're wondering whether or not He's even there. And it must be specific—not just, "Well, sure, I believe *something's* out there… Buddha, Allah, little green men." That doesn't cut it. This God we're talking about pleasing here is the One named Jehovah, the Lord Jesus Christ, and no other.

Secondly, we must believe that God is faithful to reward those who diligently seek Him. Not that He's some impersonal, mystical force in outer space, but a Person intimately interested in our day-to-day lives. Remember, faith comes by hearing the Word of God (Romans 10:17)—so diligently seek Him in it!

❧ *Day 239* ❧

"So Jesus answered and said to them, 'Have faith in God. For assuredly, I say to you, whoever says to this mountain, "Be removed and be cast into the sea," and does not doubt in his heart, but believes that those things he says will be done, he will have whatever he says. Therefore I say to you, whatever things you ask when you pray, believe that you receive them, and you will have them.'"

Mark 11:22-24

Many people misconstrue this passage into a "name it, claim it" formula, as if God is a cosmic butler to serve us at beck and call so long as we "believe." So when faced with a life-storm, they pray to that proverbial mountain, "Be cast into the sea," and when it doesn't happen immediately, they say, "Well, this Word of Faith stuff must not be real."

The issue is, most often, they forget Verse 22 in their eagerness to quote Verses 23-24. "Have faith in God." The faith isn't supposed to be in the mountain being cast into the sea—rather in the One who has the ability to cast the mountain into the sea. So the "whatever things you ask" is directly tied into those things lining up with the Word of God, which is His revealed will concerning us. (1 John 5:14-15) When we know they are lined up, we can believe that we receive them, and we will have them.

Day 240

"So Jesus answered and said to them, 'Have faith in God. For assuredly, I say to you, whoever says to this mountain, "Be removed and be cast into the sea," and does not doubt in his heart, but believes that those things he says will be done, he will have whatever he says. Therefore I say to you, whatever things you ask when you pray, believe that you receive them, and you will have them.'"

Mark 11:22-24

Now, again, I find nowhere in the Bible that it is God's will for us to suffer incessantly, impoverished, sickly and weak. So questioning God's will concerning a covenantal right as outlined in the Word of God is pretty much the opposite of "have faith in God."

But I also find nowhere that it says we'll never have contrary circumstances, trials, tribulations, or a fight on our hands to see the blessings of God manifested in our life-storms. Still, that does not change the truth: your faith in God is rewarded by having the things you ask, when you know they're in line with His Word and asked with the correct motivation. (James 4:3)

Faith in God comes by hearing the Word of God, right? Knowing God's will comes by knowing the Word of God. Once those two components are in place, we are in a position to say to "this mountain," and see it happen.

"For with God nothing will be impossible."

Luke 1:37

*T*he angel Gabriel made this statement to Mary when he informed her she would conceive the Messiah, very God Himself. It was in the context of Mary asking how she would be able to conceive as a virgin, and Gabriel answered her question while providing a double proof that "nothing will be impossible" when it comes to what God has set in motion. Not only would Mary herself conceive supernaturally, so had her cousin Elizabeth in her old age. Mary's faith was corroborated by Gabriel's double revelation, so that she said, "Let it be to me according to your word."

Our faith can be bolstered by seeing God's promises fulfilled in the lives of others. God is supernatural toward all those who pursue Him in equal measure—He is no respecter of persons. (Acts 10:34) What is available to one in the name of shelter from the storms is available to all who believe that with Him, "nothing will be impossible." If you see God moving on someone else's behalf, be completely convinced He will do the exact same for you! Let your faith be reinforced with this truth and proclaim, "Let it be to me…"

✺ *Day 242* ✺

"For with God nothing will be impossible."

Luke 1:37

*E*verything that is set forth in His Word, every promise and provision that is in line with His revealed character—these are the things that "nothing will be impossible." Of course God will never act contrary to His nature, which is inherently flawless. Many times, it seems to me that many Christians are looking for "God's will" in their lives, and most definitely there are situations and decisions that have to be made which are *not* explicitly stated in the Bible. For those times, seeking "God's will" is exactly what we should do. Storms can arise out of these situations, and we will need to seek God's wisdom on how to move past them. Yet, even in those circumstances, we can be assured God *will* provide shelter from the storms.

For the promises outlined in the written Word, we have no need to "seek God's will" for those. His will is His Word, and it's already established, ratified by Christ's crucifixion and resurrection, and executed by His indwelling Spirit working through us. In these instances, shelter from the storms is *already* provided; we simply have to appropriate that Word in our lives, and we will truly come to know that, in Him, nothing is impossible.

❧ *Day 243* ❧

"For we walk by faith, not by sight."

2 Corinthians 5:7

*T*he word for "walk" in the Greek is a compound that can be rendered "to tread all around, trample about." (Strong's #G4043) It conveys the "proof of ability to walk at large." Not just a quick jaunt down the block, but *walking* farther and farther, a long, long trip, a walkabout. For the Hebrews, the word gives a figurative image of how one "regulates one's life" or how one "conducts one's self" along the path of their life.

Paul inserts this phrase into his discourse on the resurrection of the dead, stating that the Spirit was given by God as a guarantee ("down payment, earnest") of this assurance of eternal life. (Verse 5) His intention is to show that a "faith walk" is a lifestyle—throughout the entire course of your life, from the starting place to the destination, on and on, till we receive the assurance at the end of this long journey: a life eternal with Christ Jesus. You're in pursuit of shelter from the storm for the long haul, and God has provided that shelter from beginning to end (and into eternity beyond.) Walk it by faith.

❧ *Day 244* ❧

"For we walk by faith, not by sight."

2 Corinthians 5:7

*T*he word for "sight" (Strong's #G1491) is also translated *shape, fashion,* or *appearance* in the New Testament. It speaks of the outward form of how something looks, the figure an object presents as it "strikes the eye." (*Thayer's Greek Lexicon*) The root of the word is often translated *know* or *behold*—to perceive something and then make a decision about it. It means "how something looks," to be aware of it.

We are told *not* to "walk" about our lives after this fashion. That doesn't mean we're not actually "seeing" the negative circumstances in our lives—they are perceived by the "eyes" as real, having a particular shape or appearance. But we don't walk our lives using that information to dictate our actions. Those appearances can change. Rather, we are to perceive the shape of negative circumstances through the lens of faith, understanding that we are never walking alone. Our Lord walks with us by the help of the Holy Spirit of promise. (Acts 2:33) You do not have to walk solely by what your eyes show you—you can walk by faith and see those perceptions change as God walks beside you through the storms of life.

ᘒᕽ Day 245 ᕽᘒ

"…That you may walk worthy of the Lord, fully pleasing Him, being fruitful in every good work and increasing in the knowledge of God; strengthened with all might, according to His glorious power, for all patience and longsuffering with joy…."

Colossians 1:10-11

Paul's prayer for the Colossians should be our heart's desire as well: to "walk worthy of the Lord." That is how we secure the shelter from the storms we face. We know that without faith it's impossible to please Him (Hebrews 11:6), so how we walk worthy, "fully pleasing Him," is to walk by faith, as the previous entry discussed. Walking in faith as a lifestyle is one of the primary keys to being fruitful in every good work, and as we walk with Him through life's stormy patches, we increase in our knowledge of Him—His faithfulness, holiness, miracle-working power, all the things that make up His perfect character.

The ability to walk by faith is "according to His glorious power"—it is through the help of the Holy Spirit that we are able to walk worthy; it cannot be achieved in our own strength. Finally, because of that indwelling power of the Spirit we are able to secure patience and longsuffering during the storms of life, even being joyful!

"…That you may walk worthy of the Lord, fully pleasing Him, being fruitful in every good work and increasing in the knowledge of God; strengthened with all might, according to His glorious power, for all patience and longsuffering with joy…."

Colossians 1:10-11

*T*he Greek word for *knowledge* (Strong's #G1922) is a compound word comprised of the preposition "above" and "knowledge." It speaks of "precise and correct knowledge." That is, *full discernment* concerning the divine attributes of God, "becoming acquainted with, to know thoroughly." I've heard theologians define this word as knowing something through experience. It's not just head-knowledge, but it's knowledge that you have gained by spending time with the Lord, experiential knowledge. It speaks of divine revelation from Him to you that is known in-depth from your spirit, out into your mind and emotions, then expressed through your five senses. Real knowledge. The ability to be "strengthened with all might" and infused with His "glorious power"—to have joy, patience, long-suffering in the midst of the storms of life—is directly related to the level of revelation you have concerning God's character toward you. This knowledge is increased throughout your lifetime spent with the Lord.

"But let all those rejoice who put their trust in You; let them ever shout for joy, because You defend them; let those also who love Your name be joyful in You. For You, O Lord, will bless the righteous; with favor You will surround him as with a shield."

Psalm 5:11-12

"Put their trust" means "to flee for protection, to seek refuge." (Strong's #H2620) This verse tells us that we are to rejoice because we put our trust in Him. Why are we told to rejoice? Because God *defends* us. That literally means God "covers" us. (Strong's #H5526) The word conveys the thought of being "hedged about, fenced in, shut up, overshadowed, screened." It also can mean "joined together," or "interweaved" like one would weave the boughs of a hedge together to construct a fence.

Remember that God defends those who put their trust in Him. As we face contrary circumstances, we can be assured that as we continually flee to Him for protection, He will raise a hedge of defense around us, quite literally providing shelter from the storm. Since we have chosen to trust Him, we should rejoice because we are assured that in Him we can weather any situation and come through it to victory. Shout for joy!

"But let all those rejoice who put their trust in You; let them ever shout for joy, because You defend them; let those also who love Your name be joyful in You. For You, O LORD, will bless the righteous; with favor You will surround him as with a shield."

Psalm 5:11-12

*W*ho are the righteous? It means those who are just, lawful, correct in the way they live their lives. (Strong's #H6662) The root of the word stems from "a straight path," to be stiff and rigid. This passage of scripture declares that those who put their trust in the Lord—those who love His name—are the ones who are righteous. Not only is God's defense a primary reward of putting our trust in Him, which in and of itself makes it worthwhile to follow His decrees; but it yields to us a reason for rejoicing, to shout for joy in the midst of difficult circumstances. We can be joyful because we have peace with the Lord. Thus, righteousness and peace go hand-in-hand. (See Hebrews 12:11.) With that peaceful righteousness comes rejoicing, and out of that joyful expression comes *favor* (Strong's #H7522), which is defined as "delight, pleasure, desire, acceptance, goodwill." It means to be satisfied in the Lord. His goodwill toward us is a shield against the storms of life!

❧ *Day 249* ❧

"Let love be without hypocrisy. Abhor what is evil. Cling to what is good. Be kindly affectionate to one another with brotherly love, in honor giving preference to one another; not lagging in diligence, fervent in spirit, serving the Lord; rejoicing in hope, patient in tribulation, continuing steadfastly in prayer; distributing to the needs of the saints, given to hospitality."

Romans 12:9-13

This is one of best definitions for Christian behavior in the entire Bible. It restates the two great commandments found in Matthew 22:37-40: loving the Lord with all your heart, soul, mind and strength, and loving your neighbor as yourself. We should know by now that any shelter from the storm the Lord provides for us is based on our execution of these two prime mandates. To the level that our love of God is without hypocrisy (abhorring what is evil, clinging to what is good), and to the level that we prefer one another in brotherly love, is the level that we are able to receive God's defense in the midst of trying circumstances.

Make sure, as you face the storms of life, that your sole motivation is to fulfill the law of Christ (Galatians 6:2) in these two key directives—out of that will spring every form of God's favor to carry you through your trials.

❧ *Day 250* ❧

"Let love be without hypocrisy. Abhor what is evil. Cling to what is good. Be kindly affectionate to one another with brotherly love, in honor giving preference to one another; not lagging in diligence, fervent in spirit, serving the Lord; rejoicing in hope, patient in tribulation, continuing steadfastly in prayer; distributing to the needs of the saints, given to hospitality."

Romans 12:9-13

This passage highlights several keys that we can implement in our daily lives to fulfill the two great commandments. Firstly, we are told not to lag in diligence but to be fervent in spirit serving the Lord. There is an element of attentive obedience, fervency in action, when we are waiting upon the Lord, an eager expectation to receive from Him as we minister to Him. Secondly, we are told to rejoice in hope and be patient in tribulation, consistently staying in prayer. Prayer and rejoicing are two keys of gaining patience. And lastly, we are told to be hospitable toward others, taking care of the needs of those around us in charity.

This is not some formula, some set of magical rules, to get God to act on our behalf; but they are principles of behavior that unlock the favor of God, the shelter we are seeking in the midst of stormy circumstances.

⟡ *Day 251* ⟡

"Therefore you now have sorrow; but I will see you again and your heart will rejoice, and your joy no one will take from you. And in that day you will ask Me nothing. Most assuredly, I say to you, whatever you ask the Father in My name He will give you. Until now you have asked nothing in My name. Ask, and you will receive, that your joy may be full."

John 16:22-24

Jesus was addressing His disciples in this passage, offering a prophetic prediction that after they had seen Him in His resurrected state, absolutely nothing, no one, would be able to take their joy from them. Their faith in His resurrection would carry them the rest of their lives, no matter what trials and tribulations they would face. This prophecy was true—we find nowhere in the Bible that one of His apostles ever doubted the cause for their joy after seeing their Lord and King resurrected.

Our hearts should rejoice, too, and no one should be able to steal our joy. Our faith in Christ's resurrection and ascension should be unshakably firm, such that "in that day" we will ask Him nothing. Our questions will seem inconsequential to the reward of our faithfulness: seeing our resurrected Lord just as the apostles did. Amen.

❧ Day 252 ❧

"Therefore you now have sorrow; but I will see you again and your heart will rejoice, and your joy no one will take from you. And in that day you will ask Me nothing. Most assuredly, I say to you, whatever you ask the Father in My name He will give you. Until now you have asked nothing in My name. Ask, and you will receive, that your joy may be full."

John 16:22-24

And while Jesus told Doubting Thomas, "Blessed are they who believe who have not seen," (John 20:29) His follow up statement in the above passage shows that it isn't His intention for only the disciples living at that time to have unshakeable joy because they were the privileged few to see Him bodily after His resurrection. His ascension power is to be resident in *every* believer. Just like the First Century apostles, we too have the right to ask the Father in Jesus' name for any of those provisions provided by the Lord's death so that our joy may be full.

Please don't wait until you meet Jesus face-to-face to start believing that what you ask in His name will be granted by the Father to you. Perhaps you are in a state of "until now you have asked nothing." Let me encourage you: "Ask, and you will receive!" (See 1 John 5:15.)

❧ Day 253 ❦

"…Whom having not seen you love. Though now you do not see Him, yet believing, you rejoice with joy inexpressible and full of glory, receiving the end of your faith—the salvation of your souls."

1 Peter 1:8-9

*T*hese verses are tied into the discourse of the "genuineness of your faith" being tested by "various trials." (Verses 6-7) Peter was firmly persuaded that even while undergoing the "fiery trial" (1 Peter 4:12) of our faith, we should "rejoice with joy inexpressible"—being *full of glory*; that is, full of the favor and power of God. Even here, it's not presented that we should just believe without ever having any recompense for our faith. Yes, the *end* of our faith is to be the salvation of our immortal souls (spirits, rather) when we meet our Lord face-to-face. However, the *walk* of faith (the life lived in faith) is supposed to be lived with rejoicing and glorious power.

Salvation (Strong's #G4991) is an all-inclusive word that means "deliverance, preservation, safety, health." And note it is the "*present possession* of all true Christians." Of course there is a future fulfillment, but we are experiencing salvation in the *now* by being "full of glory" through the empowering Spirit of God, and we should "rejoice with joy inexpressible."

✦ Day 254 ✦

"…Whom having not seen you love. Though now you do not see Him, yet believing, you rejoice with joy inexpressible and full of glory, receiving the end of your faith—the salvation of your souls."

1 Peter 1:8-9

Souls (Strong's #G5590) is where we get the English word *psyche*, and it comes from a root meaning "breath." It is elsewhere translated in the Bible as "heart," "mind," and "life." It is distinguished from *spirit* (Strong's #G4151), which is the immortal soul that goes to heaven or hell when a person dies. The point here is that salvation is also supposed to be a condition of our present-day, earthly souls—our mind, will and emotions, not *just* our immortal spirits when we die. Your faith in loving your unseen Lord yields rewards in your earthly life now as much as your heavenly life sometime off in the future.

Joy (Strong's #G5479) is best rendered "cheerfulness, gladness, calm delight." *Inexpressible* (Strong's #G412) means "unspeakable" most literally. It means even when dealing with life's storms, we are so calm and cheerful, we can't even put it into words because we are full of glory, experiencing the salvation (deliverance) of our souls.

✥ *Day 255* ✥

"A merry heart does good, like medicine, but a broken spirit dries the bones."

Proverbs 17:22

*W*é can read this phrase two different ways, both connected, but with a subtle distinction. A merry heart could do us good, like medicine would do us good. That's one way of reading it: the merry heart *is* the medicine itself. But if you notice the margin next to the verse, this phrase is also suitably rendered: "a merry heart makes medicine even better." Personally, I think this is the more accurate rendering, and many theologians have commented likewise.

Medicine (Strong's #H1455) stems from a root for "pulling off a bandage," implying "cured" so that you no longer need a bandage on the wound. I think the importance of such a distinction (a merry heart working *with* a bandage, instead of the merry heart being *just* the bandage itself) shows that curing (getting well, in all senses of the word, for the mind, soul and body) is a process, not always an instantaneous miracle. Sometimes deliverance can mean to go through the storm and come out "cured" on the other side. Your merry heart makes that process work even better!

"A merry heart does good, like medicine, but a broken spirit dries the bones."

Proverbs 17:22

I wish all of God's deliverance was instantaneous. Wouldn't that be nice? But if you've been born again longer than a few months, you know that is not always the case. Pretty quickly in our walk with the Lord, we realize that He expects us to mature and deepen in our understanding of His ways—how His Word works and how to appropriate its promises for ourselves. Of course, we know His Spirit is with us every step of the way, teaching us as we remain open and malleable to His guiding hand.

Keeping a merry heart during these times is one of the keys to finding shelter from the storms of life. Without it, we run the risk of developing a "broken spirit"—that means a "wounded, or afflicted, disposition." (Strong's #H5218; #H7307) The word *merry* (Strong's #H8056) implies "showing joy"—it's important to actualize and vocalize our joy in obedience to the Word. (See Psalms 98 and 100.) Keeping ourselves in an attitude of rejoicing ensures our bones won't dry out! While we wait upon the Lord's deliverance, we need to guard our hearts against discouragement.

"Be not far from Me, for trouble is near; for there is none to help."

Psalm 22:11

*T*his is a Messianic psalm. David was prophesying the Lord's words during His passion and crucifixion. Jesus quoted Verse 1 while hanging upon the cross. (Matthew 27:46) Even our Savior, in that moment, felt His heavenly Father had left Him in the midst of His agony. It's not a sin to have these thoughts of being left "all alone" in the midst of a crisis. Very few Christians will ever undergo the kind of bodily torture Jesus faced, but that doesn't negate the mental anguish of "life storms." I believe the mental suffering Jesus faced far outweighed the physical. He had never for a moment in eternity been separated from the Father. So when God poured out His wrath upon Jesus, turning away from Him as all of humanity's sins were placed upon the innocent Lamb, no wonder Jesus "cried with a loud voice," "Why have You forsaken Me?"

But this psalm also shows that Jesus continued to trust His Father wouldn't leave Him "all alone." It is the same for us—we must remember Jesus' words: "Nor has He hidden His face from Him; but when He cried to Him, He heard." (Verse 24) Remember Deuteronomy 31:6!

❧ *Day 258* ❧

"Be not far from Me, for trouble is near; for there is none to help."

Psalm 22:11

Ibelieve it's important to recognize Jesus' plea that the Father "be not far" from Him isn't just some acknowledgment that God is everywhere at all times, so He's never "far" from us. While that's certainly true, it doesn't provide much shelter from the storm for the individual person. We need to recognize that Jesus expected the Father's divine presence to be near Him in a tangible way. It's not enough to know "God is near" (because God is everywhere), but that God is *near* to you in a personal, meaningful way. He is directly, intimately involved in your daily life and struggles.

There may be "none to help" in your current "trouble." You may be in a situation where no human being can provide that comfort and support you desperately need. But just as the Father promised His Son, "I will preserve You and give You as a covenant to the people," (Isaiah 48:9—read the whole verse) He will do the exact same for us. Never forget, "God is our refuge and strength, a very present help in trouble." (Psalm 46:1) *Very present* means, "right here, right now," abundantly available to help!

❧ *Day 259* ❧

"You will show me the path of life; in Your presence is fullness of joy; at Your right hand are pleasures forevermore."

Psalm 16:11

Presence (Strong's #H6440) stems from a root meaning "to turn and look." It's often translated "face." What's interesting to note here is that *presence* is one of those distinctive Hebrew words that is singular (a face) but with a plural ending. That's odd to English speakers. Just like the Hebrew word for God is singular (because Judaism and Christianity are monotheistic—see Deuteronomy 6:4), but *Elohim* has a plural ending.

It's not many *presences*—it's just one singular presence, but in a multiple, ever-changing expression. The face of God turned toward us is diverse, limitless, in His expression toward you and me. The reason Hebrew has these strange singular-plural nouns is to show that we, as finite humans, can never encapsulate *all* that God's presence is. We could never sum up God and His face turned toward us in one, complete definition. You and I could never exhaust the presence of God in our lives, and we can never have enough! We need more and more of His benevolent expression in an ever-increasing way. That is the essence of "shelter(s) from the storm."

❧ *Day 260* ❧

"You will show me the path of life; in Your presence is fullness of joy; at Your right hand are pleasures forevermore."

Psalm 16:11

Show (Strong's #H3045) in the Hebrew is the word for "to know (by experience.)" It means to be intimately acquainted with, to "ascertain by seeing." It's not a vague concept, but something perceived firsthand—like, we all know outer space is cold, right? But it's a different thing to *know* outer space is cold because you're an astronaut.

As we draw close to the Lord and experience His ever-growing presence in the "path of life," we come to understand the "fullness of joy." There are only two paths in life: a path of life, and a path of death. (See Matthew 7:13-14.) By staying in His presence, we can know the path of life—He'll "show" it to us, and by remaining at His right hand, we can know "pleasures forevermore" because we dwell continuously in His presence. There is comfort and happiness in following the path of righteousness, not only in the world to come, but the world of right now. When faced with difficult life-decisions, choose the narrow path of life—it's not always easy, but it's always worth it.

"As the Father loved Me, I also have loved you; abide in My love. If you keep My commandments, you will abide in My love, just as I have kept My Father's commandments and abide in His love. These things I have spoken to you, that My joy may remain in you, and that your joy may be full. This is My commandment, that you love one another as I have loved you."

John 15:9-12

The context of this passage is Jesus' discourse with the disciples concerning His departure from the earth. While that would certainly be disconcerting to the disciples, He promised that when He left, the Father and the Son would dwell inside the believer (that is, one who loved God by keeping His Word; see John 14:23), and the Father would send another Helper (the Spirit) who would bring to remembrance all Jesus had said. It is because of the indwelling of the Godhead within the spirit of the believer (or lover of God's Word) that Jesus could say, "My peace I give to you." (John 14:27)

All of this is contingent upon abiding in Christ's love. And how we can abide in His love is to keep His commandments. Shelter from life's storms is directly related to our abiding in Christ's love by keeping His commandments.

ᴥᴥ *Day 262* ᴥᴥ

"As the Father loved Me, I also have loved you; abide in My love. If you keep My commandments, you will abide in My love, just as I have kept My Father's commandments and abide in His love. These things I have spoken to you, that My joy may remain in you, and that your joy may be full. This is My commandment, that you love one another as I have loved you."

John 15:9-12

Why did Jesus speak "these things" (the conversation in John 14-15) to the disciples? To overburden them with a system of controls, to make them miserable while He skipped off to Heaven? Not in the slightest! Notice that it is *His* joy that would remain within them, so that *their* joy might be full. He was experiencing that joy and wanted to translate it to His disciples. Where did His joy spring from? He knew He was going to be tortured and murdered, all while being completely innocent of any wrongdoing. If someone had a "right" to be joyless, wouldn't that have been Christ? But rather, His full joy came from abiding in His Father's love, keeping His commandments. Jesus knew if we did the same thing, *our* joy would be full, no matter what trials we might face. His commandment for this was simple: "love one another as I have loved you." Love, joy, peace—shelter from the storms—stems from obedience to His Word.

❧ *Day 263* ❧

"For His anger is but for a moment, His favor is for life; weeping may endure for a night, but joy comes in the morning. Now in my prosperity I said, 'I shall never be moved.'"

Psalm 30:5-6

King David was no stranger to both great prosperity (in all its facets) and great despondency. He had a lot of both in his life, just like all of us. The man had slain lions, bears and giants—and hidden in caves, starving, as Saul sought to kill him. The king of Israel and the hunted prey. He did a lot of wonderful things, and did some terrible things, too. He was certainly a flawed human being—does that sound familiar? His psalms, some of the most famous pieces of literature in all history, are very emotional; sometimes he's lamenting in great anguish, sometimes he's ruling from the mountaintops, overjoyed. We, too, have all known great joy and great grief.

The key to remember, through it all, the ups and downs, is that God alone can answer every need, meet every circumstance, change every hopeless situation into an occasion for joy. Whether you're currently in the valley or on the mountain, don't make the mistake of taking your eyes off Him. A night of weeping gives way to a joyful morning with Him as your sole focus.

❦ *Day 264* ❦

"For His anger is but for a moment, His favor is for life; weeping may endure for a night, but joy comes in the morning. Now in my prosperity I said, 'I shall never be moved.'"

Psalm 30:5-6

According to Acts 13:22, David was a man after God's own heart. That's a pretty significant compliment, if you think about it. What could be a greater testament to a person's legacy than to be called "after God's own heart"? David was quick to repent and sincere in his convictions to follow wholeheartedly after his God. That's what qualified him for this description.

Our bad decisions and sins don't disqualify us from living in God's favor, provided we are quick in confessing them and sincere in our motivation to turn away from those things that would kindle His anger. Many people have a skewed view of God—He is some angry tyrant always looking to punish people who step out of line. God *can* get angry, of course—don't kid yourself that He doesn't care what you do. But for those who are after His own heart, "His favor is for life." There is *always* shelter from the storm to those who pursue Him with all their might.

✥ *Day 265* ✥

"Rejoice always, pray without ceasing, in everything give thanks; for this is the will of God in Christ Jesus for you."

1 Thessalonians 5:16-18

We know that in His presence there is fullness of joy, according to Psalm 16:11. That tells me that He is, therefore, the God of joy, which is why this passage is a command to "rejoice always" if we are in Christ Jesus. *Chairo* is the Greek for "rejoice" (Strong's #G5463)—it means "be glad, be well, thrive." The word was used as greetings and salutations to open a letter, as in "Godspeed, hail!" It speaks of being "calmly happy and well off." Re-joy. Joy and joy again.

Always is a compound word in the Greek (Strong's #G3842), literally translated "all when, every when," and is rendered "evermore" in the King James—*at all times.*

Without being "in Christ Jesus" it would be impossible for us to be calmly happy and well off at all times, so this command is not able to be fulfilled without being in the God of joy's presence always.

It is a fact that the joy of the Lord is our strength (Nehemiah 8:10), and when we shelter in place (abide) in His presence, no matter what rages on around us, we can "rejoice always" in Him.

❧ *Day 266* ❧

"Rejoice always, pray without ceasing, in everything give thanks; for this is the will of God in Christ Jesus for you."

1 Thessalonians 5:16-18

*P*ray here is in a strengthened voice, implying "with fervency, earnestly" (Strong's #G4336)—more than just wishing to God, but following through with ardency. *Really* praying. And "without ceasing" (Strong's #G89) is directly rendered "without failing, not lacking, not leaving behind, not forsaking." Both these words in the Greek imply a sense of firmness and insistency.

There is a sense of permanence, consistency, fervency in "rejoice always," "pray without ceasing," "in everything give thanks." It is *activity* on your part that God expects you to do. His *will* (Strong's #G2307) is again a strengthened form—meaning, it's not His "preference" or "He would like you to; He hopes you'll consider, pretty please, with sugar on top." It is a commandment to those who are in Christ Jesus. Since God will never command you to do something, and not empower you to do so by His Spirit, His people are really without excuse. Why does He demand this? Because He knows that His shelter from the storms takes cooperation on our part, and it's certainly worth the effort to remain "in Christ Jesus."

⊰ Day 267 ⊱

"Do not quench the Spirit. Do not despise prophecies. Test all things; hold fast what is good. Abstain from every form of evil."

1 Thessalonians 5:19-22

So by not doing those things: rejoicing, praying, giving thanks always (Verses 16-18), we risk "quenching" the Spirit. That word means "suppressing or stifling divine influence." (Strong's #G4570) It's the same word used for putting out a fire—to extinguish the work of the Holy Spirit in our lives. Which means, we start to lose that shelter from the storms.

Many people tie the concept of "quenching the Spirit" with despising prophecies, and that is absolutely correct; but the entire context here shows that not rejoicing, praying, or giving thanks always is also against the will of God for you in Christ Jesus. Paul is admonishing us to abstain from every form of evil. Part of the way we do that is through the list of commands in this passage. When we are diligent in not quenching the Spirit by following these commands, we ensure that we remain in the perfect will of God for us, which is keeping Jesus in the center of all our activities. That is how we have shelter from the storm.

❧ Day 268 ❧

"Do not quench the Spirit. Do not despise prophecies. Test all things; hold fast what is good. Abstain from every form of evil."

1 Thessalonians 5:19-22

*I*n my opinion, "do not despise prophecies" is referring to more than just the simple gift of prophecy and its operation, as in when someone gives us a prophetic word at church, for example. Rather, I believe Paul was addressing the prophetic Spirit Himself, and developing a prophetic gifting within our own lives to perceive the will of God for us. It is by yielding to the Spirit of truth that we foster a sensitivity and discernment for how the Lord wants us to operate in any given situation. That is why nurturing a prophetic spirit is so important. Without it, we can easily move out of the will of God for us by not remaining centralized in Christ Jesus through every circumstance. Of course we cannot forget the remainder of this admonition which instructs us to test all things and hold fast to that which is good. That shows me this is a process, a lifestyle of progressing in rejoicing, praying, giving thanks, and prophetic intuition. The Lord knows we won't be perfect in the execution of His will in every situation, but thankfully His grace is sufficient for us! (2 Corinthians 12:9)

❧ *Day 269* ❦

"The fear of the LORD prolongs days, but the years of the wicked will be shortened. The hope of the righteous will be gladness, but the expectation of the wicked will perish."

Proverbs 10:27-28

We've discussed elsewhere that the "fear of the Lord" is more than just being afraid of Him. The Hebraic definition (Strong's #H3374), while carrying the modern impression of *fear*, also speaks of "moral reverence, respect and piety." This passage shows fearing God actually *adds* to one's days. It is the only type of fear that benefits one's quality of life! *Prolongs* (Strong's #H3254) means "to do a thing again and again, to exceed, to add, to increase more and more."

Conversely, *wicked* (Strong's #H7563) describes "a criminal," one who is "actively and morally hostile toward God." *Shortened* (Strong's #H7114) comes from a root meaning "cut down, curtailed, docked" and it speaks of reaping a harvest. It is the same word used in Job 4:8, "Even as I have seen, those who plow iniquity and sow trouble reap the same." These kinds of people are "vexed and grieved" all the days of their lives. The point here, then, is *don't* be one of those people—fear the Lord, and He will prolong your days!

❧ *Day 270* ❧

"The fear of the Lᴏʀᴅ prolongs days, but the years of the wicked will be shortened. The hope of the righteous will be gladness, but the expectation of the wicked will perish."

Proverbs 10:27-28

Isaiah 40:31 (NIV) tells us that, "…those who hope in the Lᴏʀᴅ will renew their strength." *Hope* in the Hebrew (Strong's #H8431) comes from a root meaning "to wait in expectation." Remember how we've talked about hope being a "cord" that binds you to Jesus? The idea conveyed here is to *remain* tied up in righteousness, trusting that God will bring *gladness.* That word (Strong's #H8057) is usually translated "joy or mirth."

Conversely, once again, the *expectation* (that is, the cord that binds them) of the wicked will perish—see yesterday's definition of *wicked. Perish* means "vanish, be destroyed," most literally "wander away and get lost." (Strong's #H6) It is the basis for the Hebrew name Abaddon. (See Proverbs 27:20; Revelation 9:11, "Destruction, Destroyer.")

So these two concepts: remaining tied to God in hope, or wandering away to bleak destruction, are contrasted in this passage. Remaining, moving away. We need to shelter in place!

"And God will wipe away every tear from their eyes; there shall be no more death, nor sorrow, nor crying. There shall be no more pain, for the former things have passed away.' Then He who sat on the throne said, 'Behold, I make all things new....'"

Revelation 21:4-5

*W*ipe away every tear" is repeated from Revelation 7:17, showing that Jesus, who is in His rightful place as the Lamb at the center of the Throne, will be a Shepherd to His people and lead them to springs of the water of life. These verses echo Isaiah 25:8, which declares that God will swallow up death forever.

While the ultimate fulfillment of this wonderful promise comes at the end of this age, or rather, the beginning of the age to come (that is, the new heaven and new earth—see Verse 1), there is present-day comfort in the knowledge that, "... if anyone is in Christ, he is a new creation; old things have passed away; behold, all things have become new." (2 Corinthians 5:17) We are *already* assured of the outcome of any storm we may face in this lifetime! Hang in there, your victory is promised by the One who sits at the center of the Throne!

⊰⊱ *Day 272* ⊰⊱

"'And God will wipe away every tear from their eyes; there shall be no more death, nor sorrow, nor crying. There shall be no more pain, for the former things have passed away.' Then He who sat on the throne said, 'Behold, I make all things new....'"

Revelation 21:4-5

*D*eath in this passage (Strong's #G2288) is more than literal, physical death, the separation of the soul from the body; but also death in all its facets—that is, the power of death and all the miseries it entails because of sin. (See Hosea 13:14 and 1 Corinthians 15:55-56.) The word speaks of being separated from God in Hell. *Sorrow* (Strong's #G3997) is a strengthened form of the word that means "mourning, grief." *Crying* (Strong's #G2906) is speaking of an "outcry, clamor," as one would cry out in heartache or pain. And lastly, *pain* (Strong's #G4192) is translated for "toil, anguish, intense trouble."

These are all declared as "former things" that will have passed away when God wipes away every tear from our eyes. We are promised that all things will be made new. Take comfort in the fact that God knows the end from the beginning, He has already declared what happens when all things are made new, and your "former things" have passed away in Him!

ᗕᕈ *Day 273* ᕈᘐ

"The righteous cry out, and the LORD hears, and delivers them out of all their troubles. The LORD is near to those who have a broken heart, and saves such as have a contrite spirit."

Psalm 34:17-18

*B*y our faith in Jesus Christ's atoning work, we are declared righteous before God. (2 Corinthians 5:21) We know there is nothing on our part that can earn that righteousness; it is the gift of God (Ephesians 2:8-9) imputed to us through faith in His Son. When we are in this unique position, the above passage assures us that when we cry out, the LORD *hears* and *delivers* us out of our troubles.

The word for *hears* (Strong's #H8085) speaks of "hearing intelligently" as when a judge might "hear" a case in a matter of law. In fact, the implication is that when He hears, He obeys our call for help and comes on the scene to deliver us. The word is translated *hearken* 196 times, and *obey* or *obedient* nearly 90 times. Now, that may seem odd—God *obeying* His subjects' "summons," for lack of a better term; but really this shows His obedience to *Himself,* the One God who keeps His promises and is faithful to His Word. If He is obedient, we should be as well. Obedience provides shelter!

❧ Day 274 ❧

"The righteous cry out, and the LORD hears, and delivers them out of all their troubles. The LORD is near to those who have a broken heart, and saves such as have a contrite spirit."

Psalm 34:17-18

One of the strangest verses in all of Scripture has got to be Isaiah 45:11. "Thus says the LORD, the Holy One of Israel, and his Maker: 'Ask Me of things to come concerning My sons; and concerning the work of My hands, you command Me.'" It is mind-blowing that the Holy One, the Maker, tells us, "You command Me." As we saw yesterday, God is obedient to our cries for help; but lest we think something foolish, like "I have God on speed dial," we cannot neglect Verse 18 in this passage.

God is *near* (Strong's #H7138, "neighbor, kinfolk") to those of a *broken heart* (Strong's #7665, "shattered, broken down, wrecked, torn") who have a *contrite spirit* (Strong's #H1793, "ground into powder, pulverized into dust.") It is the crushed and broken who "command" God, not the proud and arrogant. Those who don't think they need God will not receive Him. It is when we recognize our total *need* for His help that He is obedient to our call for it.

Day 275 ๚

"Blessed are the poor in spirit, for theirs is the kingdom of heaven. Blessed are those who mourn, for they shall be comforted. Blessed are the meek, for they shall inherit the earth. Blessed are those who hunger and thirst for righteousness, for they shall be filled. Blessed are the merciful, for they shall obtain mercy. Blessed are the pure in heart, for they shall see God. Blessed are the peacemakers, for they shall be called sons of God. Blessed are those who are persecuted for righteousness' sake, for theirs is the kingdom of heaven."

Matthew 5:3-10

*T*his passage is so renowned, it almost needs no introduction. Christians and non-Christians alike are at least marginally familiar with the Beatitudes ("blessings") that open Jesus Christ's most famous sermon. And yet, these well-known proverbs are somewhat cryptic, short one-liners, packed with subtle meaning that have been mined by theologians for centuries. In the Greek, *blessed* (Strong's #G3107) is a prolonged form of a poetic word that means, "happy, well off, fortunate, supremely blessed." The effect of each of these blessings stems from the cause, or condition, of the person receiving them, again showing those who *need* God are the ones who find Him. In each instance, the seeker of shelter is promised to find it when trusting in God for salvation.

"Blessed are the poor in spirit, for theirs is the kingdom of heaven. Blessed are those who mourn, for they shall be comforted. Blessed are the meek, for they shall inherit the earth. Blessed are those who hunger and thirst for righteousness, for they shall be filled. Blessed are the merciful, for they shall obtain mercy. Blessed are the pure in heart, for they shall see God. Blessed are the peacemakers, for they shall be called sons of God. Blessed are those who are persecuted for righteousness' sake, for theirs is the kingdom of heaven."

Matthew 5:3-10

*K*ingdom of heaven (Strong's #G932, reference "basilica"), the promise of which opens and closes the Beatitudes, speaks properly of "royal" inheritance, rather than a literal kingdom. It means "the right to rule, royal authority, power and dominion." Jesus is speaking of a spiritual kingdom within the life of each type of person mentioned in the passage. This is why 1 Peter 2:19 calls us "a royal priesthood," and 1 Corinthians 6:9 speaks of inheriting the kingdom of God. Those who are poor in spirit, mourn, meek, hunger and thirst for righteousness, merciful, pure in heart, peacemakers, and persecuted for righteousness' sake enter into Christ's inheritance as King of all kings!

❧ Day 277 ❧

"Let not your heart be troubled; you believe in God, believe also in Me."

John 14:1

The first step in receiving this royal inheritance, the spiritual kingdom of heaven, is to believe in God, as simple as that sounds on surface level. But this goes beyond believing in "something" out there, just a passing acknowledgement that there's some mystical Being up in the sky. We must diligently seek Him, and Him alone. (See Hebrews 11:6.) In Matthew 12:28-34, we see how Jesus expects people to "believe in God," by quoting the two great commandments; and when the scribe responds, "Well said, Teacher!" Jesus tells him, "You are not far from the kingdom of God."

The second step to inheritance is believing that Jesus is God's Christ (Messiah.) The context of this verse is the Lord telling His disciples, "I am the way, the truth, and the life. No one comes to the Father except through Me. He who has seen Me has seen the Father." (Verses 6,9) He is telling them (and us): "Believe in God, believe also in Me." (It's imperative in the Greek.) For those who do, we have His promise, through the Holy Spirit (Verses 16,17), that the "kingdom" (royal authority) of heaven is ours!

ᔙᔥ Day 278 ᔥᔙ

"Let not your heart be troubled; you believe in God, believe also in Me."

John 14:1

*D*on't be "troubled" (Strong's #G5015) in this verse speaks of "roiling water." That is, don't be agitated and stirred up, don't be "distressed or perplexed" by doubts, don't let "inward commotion" take away your peace and calmness. Jesus is declaring He is equal with God (and in fact, IS God), and is, therefore, the Answer to every problem His children might face. He promises not to leave us orphans (Verse 18) by declaring He (and the Father and the Spirit—since They are all One) will "make Our home" (Verse 23) within us.

Do you believe this? Then you should never be troubled. *Believe* in this verse comes from the Greek word for *faith* (Strong's #G4100) and means "think it to be true." This verse is stating if you trust in God, trust in Jesus also. That's what shelter from the storm really means, trusting that Jesus is your Savior in every aspect of your life, no matter what you face. No, not everything goes your way all the time—you could see "roiling waters" all around you. But God Himself is asking you to place your confidence in Him. Entrust your wellbeing to Him!

❧ *Day 279* ❦

"Surely He has borne our griefs and carried our sorrows; yet we esteemed Him stricken, smitten by God, and afflicted. But He was wounded for our transgressions, He was bruised for our iniquities; the chastisement for our peace was upon Him, and by His stripes we are healed. All we like sheep have gone astray; we have turned, every one, to his own way; and the LORD has laid on Him the iniquity of us all."

Isaiah 53:4-6

A rguably the most famous chapter in the entire Bible, this excerpt is so packed with divine revelation as to warrant entire books being written about it. The marginalia of most Bibles outlines more than a dozen literal translations from the Hebrew that bring out the Spirit-inspired beauty of Isaiah 53.

Specifically for a devotional on "shelter from the storms," the primary objective of this passage is to show that Jesus' passion and crucifixion was for the purpose of providing *us* with a safeguard against all of the storms we deserve due to our own "iniquity." Our Lord shields us from griefs, sorrows. He restores peace and provides us with complete healing, spirit, soul and body. To accept anything less demeans all the afflictions and wounds He took upon Himself in our stead!

❧ *Day 280* ❧

"Surely He has borne our griefs and carried our sorrows; yet we esteemed Him stricken, smitten by God, and afflicted. But He was wounded for our transgressions, He was bruised for our iniquities; the chastisement for our peace was upon Him, and by His stripes we are healed. All we like sheep have gone astray; we have turned, every one, to his own way; and the LORD has laid on Him the iniquity of us all."

Isaiah 53:4-6

You are probably aware that *griefs* and *sorrows* are literally translated "sicknesses" and "pains." (See Strong's #H2483, #H4341.) *Smitten* means "struck down" (Strong's #H5221) by God with those sicknesses and pains. *Wounded* is "pierced, bored through" (Strong's #H2490), while *bruised* is "crushed, broken in pieces." (Strong's #H1792) All of this sounds absolutely horrific, and it was all for the purpose of *our* peace and healing, to bring wayward sheep back to Him.

To say that God is indifferent toward, or even worse, actively *against* humanity is to completely deny what God went through in order to restore His fallen creation into that divine shelter only He can provide. It cost Him more than we can possibly understand! Make sure you don't treat that lightly.

❧ Day 281 ❧

"But even if you should suffer for righteousness' sake, you are blessed. 'And do not be afraid of their threats, nor be troubled.' But sanctify the Lord God in your hearts, and always be ready to give a defense to everyone who asks you a reason for the hope that is in you, with meekness and fear...."

1 Peter 3:14-15

Just previously, Peter sets up this passage with the question: "And who is he who will harm you if you become followers of what is good?" (Verse 13) The apostle is showing a distinction between suffering for being good and suffering for being evil. What Peter is *not* talking about is God's children suffering for evil's sake, because "Christ also suffered once for sins." (Verse 18) Why should we, then, suffer for sins a second time?

But "even if" we find ourselves suffering for righteousness' sake—that is, the persecution and struggle that *might* come from taking a stand for Christ, doing what is right and good, versus what is easy—Peter tells us we are blessed, echoing the Lord's statement in Matthew 5:10. The focus here is not the suffering, but rather the "hope that is in you," as you put your trust in God to bless you "even if" there's trouble you're facing.

❧ *Day 282* ❦

"But even if you should suffer for righteousness' sake, you are blessed. 'And do not be afraid of their threats, nor be troubled.' But sanctify the Lord God in your hearts, and always be ready to give a defense to everyone who asks you a reason for the hope that is in you, with meekness and fear...."

1 Peter 3:14-15

This passage again echoes statements Isaiah made concerning our being "not afraid" of the world's situations (Isaiah 8:12-13)—rather, we are to "sanctify the Lord God." That means we are instructed to set Him apart from *everything* else. He is above it all, in control of it all, and nothing happens without His foreknowledge of the best way to carry you through that circumstance.

We're not told to enjoy the difficult times; that's an absurdity. But we *are* called "blessed," and are instructed not to be troubled because of "the hope that is in" us. Our fear (that is, our *concern*) should be always doing what is pleasing in His sight. When we are doing that, we have no need to be afraid of anything else. We are promised that that the Lord will carry us through to the other side, not just in the life to come, as precious as that is, but in *this* life as well. Sanctify the Lord God!

✧ *Day 283* ✧

"I sought the Lord, and He heard me, and delivered me from all my fears. They looked to Him and were radiant, and their faces were not ashamed."

Psalm 34:4-5

David opens this famous psalm with a call to "the humble" that they should magnify and exalt the Lord together with him. That is the "they" of Verse 5—those who are humble are the ones "boasting in the Lord." (Verse 2) What do the humble have to boast about? That their God delivered them from all their fears and saved them out of all their troubles. (Verse 6)

Boasting in the Lord is not the sin of self-pride. (1 Corinthians 13:1) In fact, only an unassuming person would be able to acknowledge that, apart from their God, they could never be delivered of their fears. It takes a self-effacing person to be meek enough to admit that only God is worthy of their boasting. I find this a very interesting contrast—boasting and humility wedded together.

We are in a distinctive position when we humble ourselves in the sight of the Lord, for He will exalt us so we can boast in Him. (See James 4:10.) He will deliver us from all our fears, preserve us through any trouble we might face. That's worthy of praise!

❧ Day 284 ❦

"I sought the Lᴏʀᴅ, and He heard me, and delivered me from all my fears. They looked to Him and were radiant, and their faces were not ashamed."

Psalm 34:4-5

*B*oast (Strong's #H1984) originally spoke of a clear, loud sound and came to refer to bright color, to shine forth—that is, to make a show of something. So the Hebrew word can be rendered "to shine brightly, to make a clamor," either in a positive sense, like boasting of God's goodness to the world, or in a negative sense, acting like a foolish madman. In a positive light, boasting of the Lord is what causes "them" (the humble) to become "radiant" (which in the KJV is translated "lightened." This word (Strong's #H5102) speaks of the reflection of light off a swift running stream, the sheen of flowing water in sunlight, to sparkle.

When we humble ourselves before the Lord, His face is turned toward us in favor, and the light from His face is reflected off ours. We reflect the high esteem He has toward us! With that kind of preference and approval upon us, we have no reason to be fearful or ashamed. We are *bright* in the Lord!

❦ *Day 285* ❦

"Therefore I say to you, do not worry about your life, what you will eat or what you will drink; nor about your body, what you will put on. Is not life more than food and the body more than clothing? Look at the birds of the air, for they neither sow nor reap nor gather into barns; yet your heavenly Father feeds them. Are you not of more value than they? Which of you by worrying can add one cubit to his stature?"

Matthew 6:25-27

Worry was an emotion Jesus addressed at some length—it must be an important topic. He spoke about greed, fear, and hatred; and most of us nod our heads when we read His words, agreeing that those are "bad things." Yet how many of us spend hours a day worrying about circumstances completely beyond our control and don't think *that* is equally just as bad?

Many of us allow our minds to run away with the "what if's" of life. And while that's not to be dismissive of the difficult conditions many people face, the vast majority of those "what if's" never occur. We're filling our minds with stuff that won't ever actually happen. If one of those "what if's" *do* occur, in most cases, we can't do a single thing about them anyway. So we *worry* about that, and it robs us of the present. Don't give in to worry!

❧ Day 286 ❧

"Therefore I say to you, do not worry about your life, what you will eat or what you will drink; nor about your body, what you will put on. Is not life more than food and the body more than clothing? Look at the birds of the air, for they neither sow nor reap nor gather into barns; yet your heavenly Father feeds them. Are you not of more value than they? Which of you by worrying can add one cubit to his stature?"

Matthew 6:25-27

You can control the emotion of worry with the Lord's help. I recognize there are physical and mental conditions where it's not so easy to say, "Hey, be anxious for nothing." But God wants us to come to Him about it. (See Philippians 4:6-7.) In a lot of cases, our worries are not the result of a chemical imbalance or emotional disorder—it's because it makes us *feel* like we're doing something about those negative situations, whether they've really occurred, or potentially could occur.

It seems contrary to the human condition, perhaps even flippant or detached, *not* to be worrying about things. But the Lord is clear that worrying is a waste of your time and energy, a thief that steals emotional joy and mental/physical health. Be aware when you slip into worry and combat it at all costs!

✥ *Day 287* ✥

"Unless the LORD had been my help, my soul would soon have settled in silence… In the multitude of my anxieties within me, Your comforts delight my soul."

Psalm 94:17,19

W̄e highlighted Verse 18 in the previous installment, but these two verses are worth bringing out as relates to combatting worry and anxiety. They show that on our own we are not capable of removing all fear concerning the circumstances in our lives. It takes the help of the Lord to remain in peace and contentment in the midst of storms. Without God's help, David is saying that his soul—the breath of his life (Strong's #H5315)—would have perished. (Strong's #H1749) The word for *silence* in the Hebrew means to be struck down, or struck dumb, and is compared to a similar word meaning "to be destroyed, cut off, undone." The Lord's assistance through his trials is what sustained his mental and emotional stability, indeed even his physical health.

We are in a similar position to David, requiring the Lord's assistance in order to maintain freedom from worry and doubt, to keep our breath, so to speak, so we're not struck dumb. Don't let the cares of this world silence your soul—rely upon Him!

✺ *Day 288* ✺

"Unless the LORD had been my help, my soul would soon have settled in silence… In the multitude of my anxieties within me, Your comforts delight my soul."

Psalm 94:17,19

Anxieties in the Hebrew speaks of "disquieting thoughts" (Strong's #H8312) and comes from a root implying a divided mind, branching thoughts, ambivalence—in fact, the verb form of the word is used to "lop off the boughs of a tree." In other words, in order to "prune" the rampant worrying thoughts David had, it took a special grace from the LORD.

Comforts (Strong's #H8575) means "consolation, sympathy, pity." *Delights* (Strong's #H8173) speaks of being "smeared over," putting a salve on the eyes. So, because of God's unwavering compassion toward us, He extends His comfort; that is, He smooths over our anxieties, keeping our thoughts from branching all over the place till we're overgrown with worry and doubt.

All this goes to say that with the Lord's help, we can be in a position of peaceful calm internally, no matter what rages on around us on the outside. He provides this shelter because He is sympathetic to our minds' frailties and has compassion over us.

✣ *Day 289* ✣

"Blessed is the man who trusts in the LORD, and whose hope is the LORD. For he shall be like a tree planted by the waters, which spreads out its roots by the river, and will not fear when heat comes; but its leaf will be green, and will not be anxious in the year of drought, nor will cease from yielding fruit."

Jeremiah 17:7-8

Trust and *hope* in this passage are two different things. Of note, we put our trust *in* the LORD, but our hope *is* the LORD Himself. *Trust* (Strong's #H982) speaks of being "careless, bold and confident, made to feel safe." Several translators draw the correlation between an Arabic word meaning "to throw one down on one's back, to throw in one's face." The implication, therefore, is that we cast our cares upon Him. (See 1 Peter 5:7.) We throw ourselves into His arms, believing He will catch us.

Hope (Strong's #H4009) is also translated "confidence" and "trust," but it speaks of the Person Himself; that is, the "Refuge" Himself. It's not just an ability He has, the strength to catch us in His arms; but it is His very nature, the "structure" or substance of what makes Him God, which gives us the confidence to throw ourselves upon Him. The Object of our trust is worthy of that confidence—throw yourself upon Him!

❧ *Day 290* ☙

"Blessed is the man who trusts in the Lord, and whose hope is the Lord. For he shall be like a tree planted by the waters, which spreads out its roots by the river, and will not fear when heat comes; but its leaf will be green, and will not be anxious in the year of drought, nor will cease from yielding fruit."

Jeremiah 17:7-8

Jeremiah creates a compelling metaphor for the "blessed" person who trusts in God, who is their Hope. Under the Spirit's inspiration, he likens that person to a tree which has plenty of water, thereby having no fear of becoming dried out and unfruitful, even when the heat of life comes their way. *Fear* here is literally "see" (Strong's #H7200)—the blessed person will not *see* the heat when it comes. He or she won't be swayed by it, won't give it their attention, or consider it a factor for their continued growth.

Notice this tree is *planted* by the waters, it wasn't just by happenstance, but through careful planning and cultivation. This is the same word in Psalms 1:3 and 92:13. We must take care to water our roots with the Word of God. Only by spreading those roots deep can we weather those heat waves vying for our attention. But we do *not* have to be anxious in the year of drought. Dig in!

⊰ Day 291 ⊱

"But above all these things put on love, which is the bond of perfection. And let the peace of God rule in your hearts, to which also you were called in one body; and be thankful."

Colossians 3:14-15

"All these things" encompasses the main attributes of Christlike living, versus carnal living (see Verses 5, 8-9): tender mercy, kindness, humility, meekness, longsuffering, forbearance, and forgiveness. (Verses 12-13) "All these things" are wonderful characteristics of a person walking in true communion with Christ, the embodiment and epitome of each of these virtues distilled to their most perfect measure. But above all, there is love, or as the KJV translates it, *charity*. This is the Greek word *agape* (Strong's #G26), and one of my favorite definitions of this unmatchable word is "love feasts." (See Jude 12.) Agape is a wholly biblical word, created to represent love as God is Love, perfected and complete love.

Paul calls this type of love the "bond of perfection/perfectness," and this is a compound word in the Greek, "that which bundles together" (Strong's #G4886) "the more intelligent, mentally and morally complete, most mature way." (Strong's #G5046) This is what we are told to "put on": a feast of love!

❧ *Day 292* ❦

*"**But** above all these things put on love, which is the bond of perfection. And let the peace of God rule in your hearts, to which also you were called in one body; and be thankful."*

Colossians 3:14-15

*P*utting on this perfect bond of love allows us to let the peace of God *rule* in our hearts. In the Greek, this word (Strong's #G1018) refers to "deciding or determining" the outcome of how one responds. It comes from another Greek word that describes a special "umpire" who determined the victor in the Olympic games and awarded the winner their prize. (Strong's #G1017) So by allowing God's peace to be the determiner of *how* we should respond allows us to "win the prize" and emerge victorious through any contest. Follow your peace!

But how do we follow our peace? One key is "be thankful." Here we find a compound word joining "good" with "granting favors." (Strong's #G2170) *Thankful* means to be mindful of the benevolent graciousness we receive from God. Recalling that gratuitous generosity He so freely gives puts us in the position of being umpired by that perfect peace which comes from Him alone. Love, peace, and favor work hand in hand to provide shelter from the storms of life.

⧉ *Day 293* ⧉

"Anxiety in the heart of man causes depression, but a good word makes it glad."

Proverbs 12:25

*A*nxiety is probably the best modern translation of the Hebrew word used here. (Strong's #H1674) The original King James opts to go with "heaviness," which is also appropriate, but "fear, sorrow, care, dread, concern" are all apt translations. Literally the word means "to melt" and speaks of dissolving into terror, liquified by the cares of this world till we're turned into quivering jelly. It's used to describe an "agitated" or "restless" sea. (See Jeremiah 49:23.) I'm sure you know the feeling, like you're being tossed to and fro on a roiling sea, struggling to keep your head above the water. That is "anxiety" as it's used in this proverb.

This type of anxious living creates "depression." (Strong's #H7812) Again, the old King James phrases it as "maketh a man's heart to stoop," which is very fitting as the word literally means "to bow down" and refers to "sinking down" under the roiling waves of anxiety, drowning in fear and dread, smothered and crushed by concerns. The "good word" of God's faithfulness to His promises of shelter from the storms are the only solution to the anxieties of life.

"Anxiety in the heart of man causes depression, but a good word makes it glad."

Proverbs 12:25

Thankfully, we have the "more sure word" that Peter commends to us "to heed as a light that shines in a dark place." (2 Peter 1:19) This "good word" makes our hearts *glad*. Gesenius writes that the primary idea behind this word (Strong's #H8055) "appears to be that of a joyful and cheerful countenance," and Strong compares it to an Assyrian word for "flourish." Its primary usage is "to rejoice." It's pretty much the exact opposite of *anxiety* and *depression*.

There is a state of cheerful composure, a gladness, which comes from receiving the good word that Christ brings. Not that all our problems and anxieties fizzle away to nothingness, but rather, that they are not so monumental in comparison to the "light" that comes from a vibrant relationship with Christ, the Word Himself. One of the prime keys to overcoming a lifestyle of fear and despair is found in hearing that "good word" and taking it to heart—walking out its precepts in spite of the tumultuous life surrounding us. This *power* (2 Peter 1:16) is what Peter wants to make known to his readers: the majesty and the glory of the Lord Jesus Christ.

"The LORD will fight for you, and you shall hold your peace."

Exodus 14:14

*M*oses made this statement just prior to the parting of the Red Sea and the *overthrow* (Verse 27) of Pharaoh's armies. It literally says that the LORD "shook off" the Egyptians in the midst of the sea. This famous portion of scripture closes out with the Israelites seeing the "great work" (Verse 31) God did in delivering them. A bit of an understatement. That's literally "the hand with which the LORD worked" to save, or deliver, Israel.

The point here is to show that God Himself was actively involved in their salvation. The LORD "caused the sea to go back by a strong east wind all that night." (Verse 21) His hand was present to shake off the pursuers of His people—which just happened to be in a sea that drowned them all.

When it comes to the protection of His children against oppression, the hand of the Lord is not slack (2 Peter 3:9), but an ever-present help in time of trouble. (Psalm 46:1) This isn't because you and I are such perfect people, after all the Israelites were complaining as Moses made this statement. Rather, it is for His glory and honor (see Verses 17,18), and we reap the benefits!

❧ Day 296 ❦

"The LORD will fight for you, and you shall hold your peace."

Exodus 14:14

*H*old your peace" can carry a corrective connotation—similar to saying, "Hold your tongue!" or "Be quiet!" (Strong's #H2790) Moses said this in response to the Israelites' cries in Verses 11 and 12. He instructs them, "Do not be afraid. Stand still, and see the salvation of the LORD..." God in turn said to Moses, "Why do you cry to Me? Tell the children of Israel to go forward." (Verse 15)

Being still and quiet before the Lord is a running principle we find throughout the Bible. Probably because it takes a strong element of self-control and discipline not to rant and rave when the world seems to be spinning out of control in front of us. More than this, though, is all the murmuring and complaining—which the children of Israel were guilty of numerous times—shows a lack of faith. They didn't *really* believe God would deliver them. If they had, they wouldn't have needed to be told "hold your peace." Don't be like them. When you see the enemy's army arrayed before you, stand still and see the salvation of the Lord!

✏ Day 297 ✏

"'No weapon formed against you shall prosper, and every tongue which rises against you in judgment you shall condemn. This is the heritage of the servants of the Lord, and their righteousness is from Me,' says the Lord."

Isaiah 54:17

Weapon (Strong's #H3627) is actually a very generic term, simply meaning "any object that's made" and is actually translated *stuff* elsewhere. It's the same word for *instrument* in the previous verse. It can be a weapon, or furniture, or a bag, or a cup. Anything made.

So we could render this sentence as "*nothing* made against you…" There is no scheme, no plan of attack, no weapon, no *anything* that can be formed against you that shall prosper. That word (Strong's #H6743) means "to rush over" like a river rushes over the rocks. To fall upon, make progress, advance mightily. So again, we might translate this sentence as "nothing will rush over you."

This is an astoundingly powerful promise! It holds just as true today for the children of God as it did in Isaiah's day for the children of Israel. Of course, like they did, we have conditions that must be met for this promise to be effective; but as we stand in the Lord's presence, we are assured that *nothing* shall bowl us over!

"No weapon formed against you shall prosper, and every tongue which rises against you in judgment you shall condemn. This is the heritage of the servants of the LORD, and their righteousness is from Me,' says the LORD."

Isaiah 54:17

Servants of the LORD" are the ones assured nothing formed against them will be successful. When someone speaks against them, to judge them, it is the servants who condemn the accuser. Those who have willingly sold their service to God, as Paul called himself a "bondservant" in Romans 1:1. As with most things in the dynamics of the biblical Kingdom, the economy is backward to human thinking. That the servant is the one with this kind of protection, this kind of authority to "condemn," seems strange and incompatible.

However, this special condition is called the "heritage" or *inheritance* (Strong's #H5159) of these servants. Again, a surprising statement—that servants would inherit. But keep in mind that this "righteousness" is from God Himself. It is through His grace, His goodness and power, that we have this kind of special position in His Kingdom. We are merely recipients of His favor as we continue to "sell" our service to Him. We definitely receive the better end of this bargain.

❧ *Day 299* ☙

"If any of you lacks wisdom, let him ask of God, who gives to all liberally and without reproach, and it will be given to him. But let him ask in faith, with no doubting, for he who doubts is like a wave of the sea driven and tossed by the wind. For let not that man suppose that he will receive anything from the Lord; he is a double-minded man, unstable in all his ways.

James 1:5-8

Godly wisdom is the "principal thing" according to Proverbs 4:7. That means it's the *chief* or *first* thing. (Strong's #H7225) And with all that getting of wisdom, we are to get understanding, or *discernment*. (Strong's #H998) The question, then, is how do we "get wisdom?" James here tells us to ask God for it, and He'll give it liberally, without reproach. That word (Strong's #G3679) is elsewhere translated "cast favor in one's teeth," meaning God doesn't just toss wisdom at you begrudgingly, throwing it in your face.

Rather, it is God's *intention* that His children grow in wisdom and discernment—both extremely necessary qualities to avoid as much of the storms of life as possible. He *wants* you to ask Him for wisdom. So get wisdom!

❧ *Day 300* ❧

"If any of you lacks wisdom, let him ask of God, who gives to all liberally and without reproach, and it will be given to him. But let him ask in faith, with no doubting, for he who doubts is like a wave of the sea driven and tossed by the wind. For let not that man suppose that he will receive anything from the Lord; he is a double-minded man, unstable in all his ways.

James 1:5-8

*B*ut there is a condition to "getting wisdom" from God. It must be asked for in faith, with no *doubting*. That word (Strong's #G1252) speaks of "separating oneself"—that is, *dividing* yourself by wavering, or contending with yourself in your mind. All of the promises of God are appropriated through faith without dithering back and forth in our minds.

Receiving wisdom is no different than receiving physical healing or spiritual salvation or baptism in the Holy Spirit—they are all free gifts liberally extended to us by the Father through Jesus Christ. They must be received by faith, and we must remain steadfast and resolute in that grace until we have the manifestation of what we're asking for. We play a major role in receiving shelter from the storms!

❧ *Day 301* ❧

"Jesus answered them, 'Most assuredly, I say to you, whoever commits sin is a slave of sin. And a slave does not abide in the house forever, but a son abides forever. Therefore if the Son makes you free, you shall be free indeed.'"

John 8:34-36

*J*esus shows the distinction between slavery and sonship in this passage. The Lord declared He was the Truth (John 14:6), and just prior to the above statements, He stated that the Truth sets people free. (John 8:32) Sadly, the religious leaders of His day were unable (or unwilling) to recognize Him as the embodiment of Truth—and Pilate asked Jesus to His face, "What is truth?" (John 18:38)

When someone is a slave, they're unable to make choices for themselves—they lack the freedom to decide for themselves, "What is truth?" But the Spirit of adoption (Romans 8:15) transforms the former slave into a (per)son—it's a state of being, a position, not a gender—in the household of God. (Ephesians 2:19) A son inherits all of his Father's freedom, having the resources and means of his Father's kingdom at his disposal to see the Truth. The Son makes us free to explore the Truth.

❧ *Day 302* ❧

"Jesus answered them, 'Most assuredly, I say to you, whoever commits sin is a slave of sin. And a slave does not abide in the house forever, but a son abides forever. Therefore if the Son makes you free, you shall be free indeed.'"

John 8:34-36

We've pointed out before that Jesus' name expresses the concept of "freedom," (Strong's #H3467)—set at liberty, given ample space to move about, free to explore and discover all that the Truth of the kingdom has to offer. (Romans 14:7) The Greek word for *free* here (Strong's #G1658) is a civil state of existence: "freeborn, or one who ceases to be a slave," ethically, "no longer under the yoke of the Mosaic Law." It comes from a root (Strong's #G2064) meaning "to come and to go" as one pleases. So the Son makes you *this* kind of free.

However, I want to point out that just because you have the "space to move about," there is an action on your part to *move about.* Many people who come into the kingdom often just sit in the courtyard, expecting Someone else to move them along—perhaps because they still have a "slave mentality." It's like a horse that's so used to being tethered, eventually you don't even have to tie it up. Make sure you step out into the kingdom!

⊰ *Day 303* ⊱

> *"'Bring all the tithes into the storehouse, that there may be food in My house, and try Me now in this,' says the* LORD *of hosts, 'if I will not open for you the windows of heaven and pour out for you such blessing that there will not be room enough to receive it.'"*

Malachi 3:10

Tithing is often a sore topic nowadays, but I think it is important that we recognize it is a principle biblically established by Abraham tithing of the spoils to Melchizedek. (See Genesis 14.) It was carried over into Mosaic Law (see Numbers 18) and was commended by the Lord in Matthew 23:23. This devotional is not intended to be doctrinal treatise on tithing in the modern church setting, but let us not forget that there *is* promise of blessing from God to "try" Him in this. This word in the Hebrew (Strong's #H974) speaks of "testing, trying, proving," especially related to testing the purity of a metal.

God doesn't need your money. The tithe was instituted as a means of providing for the priests and as a type of welfare system for the indigent and to protect against famine. "Storehouse" (Strong's #H686) means "to lay up treasure in a shelter." A giving heart provides shelter from the storms of life.

❧ Day 304 ❧

"'Bring all the tithes into the storehouse, that there may be food in My house, and try Me now in this,' says the LORD of hosts, 'if I will not open for you the windows of heaven and pour out for you such blessing that there will not be room enough to receive it.'"

Malachi 3:10

A giving nature is at the root of biblical blessing in all its facets, more than just monetary security, but prosperity as the Lord has it. That is, blessing without measure—which is why He says, "there will not be room enough to receive it." That's a bold statement, one that could only be made by omnipotent deity to hold any kind of validity.

But this is why Jesus commands us in Luke 6:38: "Give, and it will be given to you: good measure, pressed down, shaken together, and running over will be put into your bosom. For with the same measure that you use, it will be measured back to you." He understands the context of this statement: forgive and be forgiven, judge not and be not judged, a good tree bears good fruit, and a bad tree bears bad fruit. There is a heavenly law of reciprocity. Shelter from the storms of life is directly tied into this principle: be a cheerful giver and He will cheerfully give back more than you can hold!

❧ *Day 305* ❧

"Indeed I have all and abound. I am full, having received from Epaphroditus the things sent from you, a sweet-smelling aroma, an acceptable sacrifice, well pleasing to God. And my God shall supply all your need according to His riches in glory by Christ Jesus."

Philippians 4:18-19

*G*iving in any aspect is always a sacrifice. There's constantly something else your money, or your time, or your energy *could* go to. But when we dedicate our giving to the Lord with the right heart attitude (see 2 Corinthians 9:6-7), that sacrifice is "well pleasing to God," especially as it relates to charitable giving. This is why James 1:27 declares, "Pure and undefiled religion before God and the Father is this: to visit orphans and widows in their trouble, and to keep oneself unspotted from the world." When we operate under both conditions, it is "a sweet-smelling aroma" to Him.

As we've studied again and again in these devotionals, it is to the level that we operate as God expects us to operate that we can then expect the blessing—the shelter from life's storms—to overtake us. We cannot neglect the mandate of a giver's heart any more than we can neglect keeping ourselves unspotted from the world. They go hand in hand!

❧ *Day 306* ❧

"Indeed I have all and abound. I am full, having received from Epaphroditus the things sent from you, a sweet-smelling aroma, an acceptable sacrifice, well pleasing to God. And my God shall supply all your need according to His riches in glory by Christ Jesus."

Philippians 4:18-19

"Shall supply" (Strong's #G4137) can be rendered as "fill up to the brim" or "completely furnish." It is used in a literal sense to mean "cram a net totally full of fish." The root of the word is used to describe a hollow vessel entirely jam-packed, chockfull with no space left, and speaks of *whole grain*, not just the seed but the hull containing it as well—the whole thing.

Need (Strong's #G5532) is not necessarily *wants* or *desires*, though God does promise to give us the desires of our hearts, when they are in line with His heart's desires (see Psalm 37:4.) But here, *need* comes from the word meaning "to handle one's business" and is actually a word for "employment." It's used in this context in Acts 6:3. By Christ, God out of His infinite riches and glory, supplies everything you need to get the task done entirely, whatever that duty may be. He is the ultimate form of "job security!"

"He who overcomes shall be clothed in white garments, and I will not blot out his name from the Book of Life; but I will confess his name before My Father and before His angels."

Revelation 3:5

Each of the churches that Jesus speaks to in Revelation 2-3, He mentions "to him who overcomes." This word in the Greek (Strong's #G3528) is where we get the English word Nike, like the shoes. The names Nicholas and Victoria share the same root. It means "conquer, subdue, prevail, gain the victory over one's enemies."

In John 16:33, Jesus declares He has overcome the world, and we are told in 1 John 4:4, that because Christ is in us, *we* have overcome the world. The next chapter, 1 John 5:4-5, clarifies it's our faith that Jesus Christ is the Son of God which enables us to conquer "the world"—the primary source of all life's storms.

As we put our faith in Jesus, we become like Him. And what is He? More than anything else, He is the Victor, the Conquering One—the Son of God whom even Death could not subdue. When we grow in Him, we too overcome every storm by His blood and the word of our testimony (see Revelation 12:11.)

❧ *Day 308* ❧

"He who overcomes shall be clothed in white garments, and I will not blot out his name from the Book of Life; but I will confess his name before My Father and before His angels."

Revelation 3:5

*C*lothed in white garments" speaks of being separated from anything in the world that would taint or color the overcomer—we are promised eternal, total separation from the very presence of sin and its effects when we receive our inheritance in heaven. Isaiah 61:10 speaks of these "garments of salvation, robes of righteousness." Historically, white garments were reserved for those who were in places of honor at ceremonies—it was a mark of esteem by the host to be given a white robe to wear.

Secondly, we receive assurance that our names will never be blotted out of the Book of Life. The security offered by the white garments is everlasting and endless. Lastly, Jesus Himself, our God and King and Savior, will confess our names before the Father and His angels, meaning we will have the distinct privilege of being publicly declared "Jesus' Very Own Overcomers" before the entire host of heaven. What a thrilling ending to the storms of life—honored and acknowledged as victorious before the Creator Himself. Be an overcomer!

Day 309

"…That if you confess with your mouth the Lord Jesus and believe in your heart that God has raised Him from the dead, you will be saved. For with the heart one believes unto righteousness, and with the mouth confession is made unto salvation."

Romans 10:9-10

It isn't all that difficult to become born again by the Spirit above. There are only two conditions. However, on the other side of that truth: *there are only two conditions that will make you born again.* The plan of salvation is a simple, but very narrow, way. All other works are of no avail, only faith in one Person: the Lord Jesus Christ. God foreordained it this way on purpose, because of the great effort it cost to procure it; namely, that God would become incarnate and tie Himself to mankind for all eternity.

Shelter from the storms of life is found in exactly this same way. Only Jesus Christ can provide true, lasting protection and salvation. Everything in our own meager power is ultimately vain and fruitless. Shelter *must* be procured on God's terms, and no other. It must be accessed and walked out by faith. There are no shortcuts.

❧ *Day 310* ❧

"…That if you confess with your mouth the Lord Jesus and believe in your heart that God has raised Him from the dead, you will be saved. For with the heart one believes unto righteousness, and with the mouth confession is made unto salvation."

Romans 10:9-10

Salvation is inherently a simple idea because it was envisioned by a perfect God—it is something attainable by every person on this planet, regardless of any distinguishing factors they may have. So, if you're a human being, you can be saved. There is no "but" to that. In like manner, you can also walk in the shelter that Jesus provides. It *is* attainable by every born-again believer on this planet, no matter *what* they are facing. Again, there is no "but."

Of course, this doesn't mean life suddenly becomes super easy just because you believe in your heart and confess with your mouth that Jesus is your righteousness and salvation. Oh, how we all wish that were so! The One providing that shelter is also the One who promises you will have trials and tribulations (see John 16:33.) The difference, then, between the faith-walking person and the disbelieving person is the promise of prevailing against those adversities, and being at peace while doing so!

❧ *Day 311* ❧

"But you are a chosen generation, a royal priesthood, a holy nation, His own special people, that you may proclaim the praises of Him who called you out of darkness into His marvelous light…"

1 Peter 2:9

C hosen (Strong's #G1588) is where we derive the English word *eclectic*, which has a slightly different modern connotation than in the past. Today, the word means "a wide variety taken from a broad range." So, I have eclectic tastes in music means I like a wide variety of styles. In the Greek, the word literally means "picked out"—elected. Jesus is elected by the Father to "the most exalted office conceivable," and we are "chosen to obtain salvation through Christ." I do not take this in an ultra-Calvinistic sense—I believe anyone who would choose to come to Jesus would, in turn, be chosen by Him.

The word also applies to a specific *type* of Christian: "choice, select, i.e. the best of its kind or class, excellence preeminent." It isn't that these Christians are better than others—you're either saved or you aren't. But there will always be a core group of people who jut out a little further—those of an excellent or different spirit (see Daniel 6:3; Numbers 14:24.) That's who I want to be! Don't you?

❧ Day 312 ❧

"But you are a chosen generation, a royal priesthood, a holy nation, His own special people, that you may proclaim the praises of Him who called you out of darkness into His marvelous light…"

1 Peter 2:9

*R*oyal (Strong's #G933) comes from the root where we get the English word *basis*, or foundation—which is used to derive the word "kingly, royal" in the Greek; that is, having a strong foundation of power and authority. It's elsewhere translated "kings' courts" (Luke 7:25), meaning the royal palace. The concept of *kingly power* is then wedded to a *priesthood* (Strong's #G2406), of which Thayer defines, "so Christians are called, because they have access to God and offer not external but 'spiritual' sacrifices; priests of kingly rank, exalted to a moral rank and freedom which exempts them from the control of everyone but God and Christ." (See 1 Peter 2:5.)

We are kingly priests, which makes us *special* (Strong's #G4047)—the KJV translates it "peculiar." This word literally means "a possession, something purchased, preserved and held back for one's own property." In this case, we were *bought* by God and held by Him, reserved for His own special, peculiar use—to proclaim His praises everywhere. What a powerful portion of scripture!

✑⋆ *Day 313* ⋆✎

"My son, give attention to my words; incline your ear to my sayings. Do not let them depart from your eyes; keep them in the midst of your heart; for they are life to those who find them, and health to all their flesh. Keep your heart with all diligence, for out of it spring the issues of life."

Proverbs 4:20-23

A ttention (Strong's #H7181) is a word that means "prick up your ears"—it's used to describe an animal that becomes alert and concentrating on a sound, like when a horse, dog, or deer will prick up their ears to focus on something they've heard. The connotation is "sharpening" one's ears to focus on a sound. Likewise, *incline* (Strong's #H5186) is the same word used to describe "pitching" a tent, with the concept of "stretching or spreading out." So this sentence could be construed as "sharpen and spread your ears to concentrate on what I'm saying."

One must really pay attention to what the Bible is saying for it to be effective in one's life. Casual, cursory examination isn't enough to make God's promises of safety and security active. Only diligent hearkening to the Word will make it operative. But for those who do, His Word is guaranteed to provide life and health to them. Focus!

❧ Day 314 ❧

"My son, give attention to my words; incline your ear to my sayings. Do not let them depart from your eyes; keep them in the midst of your heart; for they are life to those who find them, and health to all their flesh. Keep your heart with all diligence, for out of it spring the issues of life."

Proverbs 4:20-23

Keeping God's Word in your head is important, but that doesn't make the Word active or fruitful in your life. That's why this passage admonishes us to *keep* (Strong's #H8104) His Word in the midst of our heart. The Hebrew word used here is also the proper name for "watchman or gatekeeper." It can mean "overseer"—and it appears to be linked to "supporting the eyelid" and talking throughout the night to stay awake. (See *Brown, Driver, Diggs' Lexicon*.) So it speaks of constant vigilance to make sure the Word doesn't "depart from your eyes."

The word *diligence* (Strong's #H4929) shares the same root as *keep*—speaking of a guardhouse or a prison. That is, "keep your heart in custody, well-guarded." *Issues* (Strong's #H8444) speaks of borders, the gates of a city—the comings and goings of life (storms.) Guard the Word to guard your heart, and keep those "issues" at the gates!

✥ Day 315 ✥

"To everything there is a season, a time for every purpose under heaven..."

Ecclesiastes 3:1

Solomon wrote a poem in Ecclesiastes 3:2-8 outlining the seeming inconsistencies of life, juxtaposing things that seem like opposites: good things, bad things, all rolled into one overall experience we call "living," with its ups and downs swirling cyclically in a system he states is "vanity." (Ecclesiastes 1:2) This word in Hebrew (Strong's #H1892) means *vapor* or *breath* and is used figuratively to mean "absurdity, frustration, futility, nonsense" (see marginalia.) While at first that may sound pretty dismal on the surface, the point of this poem, according to Verses 11, 14-15, is to show that without an understanding of God's sovereignty, foreknowledge and omniscience in planning the end from the beginning, the cycles of one's life are practically meaningless.

I often feel that the mountains and valleys are all mixed together—in some area of life, I'm on the mountaintop, in another in the valley of trial. It's usually not either/or, it's both. I take comfort in knowing that God appointed both the crest of the wave and the trough of the wave beforehand—which means He'll carry me though them both. You should be comforted, too!

❧ *Day 316* ❧

"To everything there is a season, a time for every purpose under heaven..."

Ecclesiastes 3:1

*N*othing you will ever face, good or bad, surprises God. He has appointed *all* before the world was ever fashioned. Down to the last, minute detail of your life, He was aware of it all, looking *back* at it through eternity future (to our way of thinking) so that He could then *begin* to allow His master plan to unfold. You *are* a part of that master plan. God never starts something that He hasn't already finished—this is so hard for a finite human mind to grasp, but the Bible declares this to be true.

People ask all the time, "Why does God allow bad stuff to happen?" So that His plan of ultimate good will be completed (to us—it's already finished to Him.) This life *is* a vapor, a fleeting moment, a drop of water in the infinite ocean of God's perfect existence, which you are a part of if you're in Him. That is not to demean what you are going through. In the present, it might feel utterly overwhelming. But looking at it with the eternal eyes of God's finished work, we can draw hope that the bad stuff, the good stuff, and everything in between, is a link to His completed, flawlessly charted purpose for you as an individual and the world at large.

❧ *Day 317* ❧

"...If My people who are called by My name will humble themselves, and pray and seek My face, and turn from their wicked ways, then I will hear from heaven, and will forgive their sin and heal their land."

2 Chronicles 7:14

*G*od did not create evil. It is an impossibility for Him to do or think anything "bad." (Yes, there are some things an omniscient, omnipresent, omnipotent Being *can't* do—like allow sin to go unpunished.) What He *can* do is create a being with freewill to choose evil (sin) on its own—as in the case with Lucifer and Adam and Eve. Like we saw in the previous entries, God *appointed* (demarcated an allotment of time) for all the good *and* bad things to happen. That means He *knew* Lucifer would turn on Him before He created him; He *knew* Adam and Eve would sin before He made the world. And He did it anyway to allow His master plan (His Word, Jesus Christ) to be completed.

People often declare God is unjust for fashioning a world like this. And they would be right, *if* He didn't provide a means of correcting the wrongs—that is, through the blood of His Son. If people humble themselves, seek His face, turn of their own volition from their evil ways, He *will* forgive them... and heal their land.

Day 318

"…If My people who are called by My name will humble themselves, and pray and seek My face, and turn from their wicked ways, then I will hear from heaven, and will forgive their sin and heal their land."

2 Chronicles 7:14

This statement was given to Solomon after he had prayed and dedicated the temple, and all Israel kept the feast with him, so that the Lord's glory filled the temple and His fire consumed the sacrifices made in His name. (See Verses 1-11.) This promise was made in the context of God also declaring, "When I shut up heaven and there is no rain, or command the locusts to devour the land, or send pestilence among My people…" (Verse 13) All these "bad things" are a result of sin, not God being a petulant tyrant. Yes, He *appointed* them, but He also appointed the promise: "If my people… then I will…"

I'd like to think this encounter helped Solomon with his "vanity" dilemma—it added *meaning* to the ups and downs he saw in life. When we accept as true that God is just and merciful, righteous and gracious, in a perfectly balanced measure, and that He has accounted for every moment of our life, we can be comforted in knowing He keeps His promises to carry us through the storm.

❧ *Day 319* ❦

"Now as Jesus passed by, He saw a man who was blind from birth. And His disciples asked Him, saying, 'Rabbi, who sinned, this man or his parents, that he was born blind?' Jesus answered, 'Neither this man nor his parents sinned, but that the works of God should be revealed in him.'"

John 9:1-3

*J*esus makes it clear in this instance that sin was not the reason behind this beggar's blindness—neither his own sin nor his parents'. Of course, we should know that sin *can* carry consequences resulting in health issues and poverty (see John 5:14); sometimes the reason *is* unconfessed sin. However, we all need to be extremely careful in assigning blame for negative circumstances in someone's life. Here we see Jesus did not do so. Not always is illness or poverty a result of whether we sin or not. This is why Jesus states, "…for He makes His sun rise on the evil and on the good, and sends rain on the just and on the unjust." (Matthew 5:45)

When faced with trials and attacks, it can be wise to ask the Holy Spirit to show us if there is unconfessed sin that has opened the door. But also recognize not all of life's storms are due to sin. Regardless, we should expect the "works of God" to be revealed in us.

❧ Day 320 ❧

"Now as Jesus passed by, He saw a man who was blind from birth. And His disciples asked Him, saying, 'Rabbi, who sinned, this man or his parents, that he was born blind?' Jesus answered, 'Neither this man nor his parents sinned, but that the works of God should be revealed in him.'"

John 9:1-3

The point Jesus was making here was *Himself,* not assigning blame for sin—because *everyone* was guilty of sin, except Him. Only through Him would the complete works of God be revealed: the obliteration of sin's effects. Blindness itself, which was the result of comprehensive sin worldwide, was subjected to Christ's authority, given to Him by the Father. In the history of the Bible up to that point, no one had ever been healed of blindness. That particular miracle was reserved for that moment in time to prove that Jesus is the Light of the world. (Verse 5) God had foreordained that moment in eternity past.

Our focus should not be on earthly trials—it should be on Christ as our Light. Because of our relationship to Him, the effects of sin start to become undone, bringing us closer and closer to the perfected shelter from the world that Jesus provides. That should be our primary focus!

☙ Day 321 ❧

"'I have seen his ways, and will heal him; I will also lead him, and restore comforts to him and to his mourners. I create the fruit of the lips: peace, peace to him who is far off and to him who is near,' says the LORD, 'and I will heal him.'"

Isaiah 57:18-19

*H*e in this passage refers to a person of "contrite and humble spirit." (Verse 15) God states He was angry because of "his" (that is, everyone's) sin and hid Himself from him—leaving him open to the storms of life. God "struck" him out of anger. Sadly, it also states that he "went on backsliding in the way of his heart." (Verse 17) Anger wasn't the answer. Even when the effects of sin struck, all it did was make "him" pull away from God more. Sin corrupts completely. In other words, remaining angry and allowing mankind to be swallowed up in sin while God hid Himself away didn't solve the problem. The only thing that could fix this situation is if God *healed* him.

So God pledged to revive the spirit and the heart of those who *wanted* to change their ways, and couldn't in their own power. But when we humble ourselves and come to Him, He promises to lead us out of those storms into "peace, peace."

☙ *Day 322* ❧

"'I have seen his ways, and will heal him; I will also lead him, and restore comforts to him and to his mourners. I create the fruit of the lips: peace, peace to him who is far off and to him who is near,' says the Lord, 'and I will heal him.'"

Isaiah 57:18-19

Note that God declares He creates "the fruit of the lips." Grace and restoration originate with Him, just as does love. (See 1 John 4:19.) Whether we take this to mean *irresistible grace* (as in Calvinism) or *prevenient grace* (as in Arminianism) or some variation thereof, nearly universally all Christians believe the concept of grace finds its source in God. It is He who initiated the means by which mankind could approach Him, through His Son Jesus Christ.

Whether we are far off or near, God is offering peace to mankind through the New Covenant. Peace in all its facets, which encompasses everything when we say "shelter from the storm." Those who "mourn" and humble themselves are invited to restored comforts—security, stability, divine protection—in the healing that God provides. It all started with Him, and it all ends with Him. We must simply accept that grace by faith and work with Him as He revives the spirit and the heart. Amen.

❧ *Day 323* ❧

"Behold, I will bring it health and healing; I will heal them and reveal to them the abundance of peace and truth."

Jeremiah 33:6

*H*ealth (Strong's #H724) is an interesting word in the Hebrew. It's closely akin to "restoration," most properly meaning the new skin that grows at a wound site 3633and can refer to the long bandages a physician uses to treat an injury, according to Gesenius. This is because it's related to the word for "prolong, lengthen" (Strong's #H748), which was used to describe stretching out tent cords in order to erect shelter; though it often refers to time, as in "prolonging one's days."

According to God's statement here, an abundance of truth and peace is used to restore one to health—to make the new skin grow over an injured area, to lengthen one's days. This is in the context of God returning Israel and Judah from captivity, admonishing them to, "Call to Me, and I will answer you, and show you great and mighty things, which you do not know." (Verse 3) Truth and peace are great and mighty things that God is offering to His people when they call to Him. He will erect shelter from the storms around your life—what a great promise!

❧ *Day 324* ❧

"Behold, I will bring it health and healing; I will heal them and reveal to them the abundance of peace and truth."

Jeremiah 33:6

*H**ealing* (Strong's #H4832) is a different word than "health" here. It comes from the root for the covenantal name of God, Jehovah Rapha, which in turn means the Physician, or literally "the One who mends by stitchwork." (Strong's #H7495) The word for healing when used concretely means "medicine, a cure," and it's used in this passage to mean "deliverance." So again, the abundance of peace and truth that God reveals yields freedom from the tyranny of oppression in a literal, physical sense.

However, there is an abstract sense to the word that speaks of soundness of mind, placidity, tranquility. When God delivers, He also restores mental serenity as well. This word speaks of a refreshing for the mind as well as the body, a total working of restoration from the catastrophes arising out of the storms of life. Lastly, this word refers to composure of speech, a serene tongue, the softness of words. God also removes the bitterness that comes from facing life's storms, restoring a complete person to total liberty in every facet of life.

❧ *Day 325* ❧

"The LORD will deliver him in time of trouble. The LORD will preserve him and keep him alive, and he will be blessed on the earth; You will not deliver him to the will of his enemies. The LORD will strengthen him on his bed of illness; You will sustain him on his sickbed."

Psalm 41:2-3

*D*eliver (Strong's #H8104) properly means "to hedge about as with thorns," and as we mentioned in a previous entry, is the word used for "watchman." Deliverance here speaks of preservation and protection—being carried through difficulties and kept alive. "Blessed on the earth" (Strong's #H833; #H776) is interesting. The first Hebrew word literally means "to go straight on"—to be "level, right, happy" in one's walk through life. The second word for "earth" means "the ground," and it appears to stem from a root meaning "to be firm." The phrase is conveying the idea of being level and firm, not out of plumb and inconsistent.

Following the Lord does not mean there is no "time of trouble." The sin principle operating on the earth, while paralyzed by the triumph of Jesus on the cross, will only be removed upon His second coming. But in the meantime, He *does* promise to carry us through it and be blessed while upon the earth!

ॐ Day 326 ᛒ

"The LORD will deliver him in time of trouble. The LORD will preserve him and keep him alive, and he will be blessed on the earth; You will not deliver him to the will of his enemies. The LORD will strengthen him on his bed of illness; You will sustain him on his sickbed."

Psalm 41:2-3

Where we are *not* delivered to is unto the will of our enemies. Both words for *will* and *enemy* in the Hebrew (Strong's #H5315, #H341) appear to stem from the idea of "drawing breath." They speak of "blowing, puffing, huffing in anger." (Gesenius) So the idea conveyed here is that the Lord will not turn us over to the desires and machinations of someone who hates us—those who are enraged against us, wishing to do us harm.

Strengthen (Strong's #H5582) speaks of nursing back to health, feeding someone who's sick in bed so they recover strength: comfort, sustain, support. The idea is given of propping someone up with your forearm. *Sustain* (Strong's #H2015) literally means "to turn over, overturn," and is used for "making a bed." Again, this word shares the idea that God nurses us back to health, changing our sheets, bringing comfort and nourishment until a change is affected and we are "turned over" once again in health. What a great promise!

☙ *Day 327* ❧

"The preparations of the heart belong to man, but the answer of the tongue is from the LORD. All the ways of a man are pure in his own eyes, but the LORD weighs the spirits. Commit your works to the LORD, and your thoughts will be established."

Proverbs 16:1-3

*H*umans have a tendency to believe their thoughts and actions are always correct, and many well-meaning Christians take this passage as saying their plans are "backed up" by God. Since they are Christians, they believe everything they "dream up" is inspired by God. But these scriptures are saying that it's reversed. It's inspired by God and *then* they dream it up. We need to "commit our works" to God and *then* our thoughts will be established (made to work out.)

God does prosper our "preparations"—but only after He has weighed our spirits; that is, judged the heart motivation *behind* the plans. We need to understand that only what originates within the heart of God will bear lasting fruit. The idea conveyed here is not "think up whatever you want, and God will make it work out." That is the misconception of a "name it, claim it" theology. Rather, what God thinks up will work out, and as we commit ourselves to Him, His thoughts become ours.

✤ Day 328 ✤

"The preparations of the heart belong to man, but the answer of the tongue is from the LORD. All the ways of a man are pure in his own eyes, but the LORD weighs the spirits. Commit your works to the LORD, and your thoughts will be established."

Proverbs 16:1-3

Committing our works to the LORD is a lifestyle process of sanctification unto Him alone. The less worldliness we have, the more our preparations become His provisions, and the more our thoughts will become established. That's not to say thinking and making plans is evil; God gave each person a mind and will to be "subcreators." But He intends for each person to renew their mind and submit their will to Him in an ever-increasing relationship with Jesus and His Word.

Part of the shelter that God provides from life's storms comes from that commitment to yield our soulish life to Him, and then our ideas and plans line up with His pre-determined ideas and plans. (That means they were all His ideas and plans to begin with.) That's how the "answer of the tongue" comes from the LORD. Not that we came up with something, and He made it work out—but rather, that He came up with something, and we were in tune enough with Him to think as He does.

⋙ Day 329 ⋘

"So you shall serve the LORD your God, and He will bless your bread and your water. And I will take sickness away from the midst of you."

Exodus 23:25

A covenant of divine healing between God and His followers is a distinction that separates Christianity from other world religions, the majority of which teach that sickness and disease are tools used to create faith in their respective deities or to impart humility through suffering. That kind of philosophy has sadly crept into Christianity and is one of the most prevalent heresies extant today.

But the Judeo-Christian religions have *always* been rooted in divine healing and health from the outset. Yahweh made it clear from His earliest revelations that He is a God who heals physical ailments. Modern Christianity has tried to downplay that element of God's nature, either by claiming He has changed His stance toward it, or that He deals primarily with mental and emotional wellbeing, choosing to exclude physical healing in most cases. Yet, this verse makes it very clear—the very physical necessities of bread and water are tied into taking sickness away from those who "serve the LORD your God."

❊ Day 330 ❊

"So you shall serve the LORD your God, and He will bless your bread and your water. And I will take sickness away from the midst of you."

Exodus 23:25

Covenants are, of course, conditional; meaning, certain conditions must be met for the covenantal agreement to be honored. The covenant of healing is no different: it is conditional upon *if* and *then*. If God's statutes are followed (Exodus 15:26), and we serve Him with all our heart, soul, mind and strength (Deuteronomy 6:1), then we are told that sickness will be taken away from us, and our physical needs (the bread and water issues of life) will be taken care of.

The highest level of execution for this covenant would be walking in divine health (see Psalm 105:37) and divine provision (see Deuteronomy 8:4), but it is still a wonderful blessing from God that He provides shelter *through* the storm of sickness as well, a promise to restore us through the process of divine healing. While we have conditions that must be met, and we have a role to play in it, we must always keep in mind that divine healing at its source is an act of mercy on God's part, rooted in His unfailing grace.

❧ *Day 331* ❦

"...He made a statute and an ordinance for them, and there He tested them, and said, 'If you diligently heed the voice of the LORD your God and do what is right in His sight, give ear to His commandments and keep all His statutes, I will put none of the diseases on you which I have brought on the Egyptians. For I am the LORD who heals you.'"

Exodus 15:25-26

*S*tatute (Strong's #H2706) stems from a root for "engrave" or more properly "to hack or cut into." In other words, a law carved in stone. It refers to a decree that is "established and definite," a commandment that we're expected to adhere to, not a polite suggestion, if we want to. *Ordinance* (Strong's #H4941) is the judgment rendered in a lawsuit, a sentencing, and is translated "regulation" in the marginalia. Again, implying a settled matter, there's no more discussion accepted about it.

The point to make here is that the provisions of divining healing and health are not capable of being changed, they're decrees that God has passed down to His people, forever settled as if written in stone. But likewise, the conditions for receiving those provisions are also not open to further debate. They either are met, or they're not. There's no halfway with God.

❧ *Day 332* ☙

"…He made a statute and an ordinance for them, and there He tested them, and said, 'If you diligently heed the voice of the LORD your God and do what is right in His sight, give ear to His commandments and keep all His statutes, I will put none of the diseases on you which I have brought on the Egyptians. For I am the LORD who heals you.'"

Exodus 15:25-26

God used this statute of "if, then" concerning divine healing and health to *test* the Israelites. That word (Strong's #H5254) means "to put to the test, to prove." According to Gesenius, this word carries a slightly different connotation than testing something by touching it, but rather to test something by smelling it. Does it pass the smell test? Is something a little fishy, has it gone off, does it stink? In other words, disobedience reeks to the LORD.

Notice, the pledge here doesn't *test* God. It's not a matter of trying to see if He'll keep His end of the bargain. He *is* the Lord who heals us, that's carved in stone. The point of this covenant promise is to see if our obedience is genuine and sincere—or does it stink to high heavens? Does our obedience pass the smell test, or are we just trying to "get something" from God?

❧ *Day 333* ❦

"Bless the LORD, O my soul, and forget not all His benefits: who forgives all your iniquities, who heals all your diseases, who redeems your life from destruction, who crowns you with lovingkindness and tender mercies, who satisfies your mouth with good things, so that your youth is renewed like the eagle's."

Psalm 103:2-5

Benefits (Strong's #H1576) means "dealing of the hands" and comes from the root word used for weaning a baby. It can speak of fruit ripening. The idea conveyed here is "dealing with something fully," showing growth and development, so a reward is bestowed for something well done.

As we grow and mature in our relationship with God, there are benefits, recompense and reward, for developing in His ways. There are many advantages to walking with the Lord: forgiveness of sin, healing from physical diseases, redemption out of the storms of life, being crowned with lovingkindness, even our basic needs being met, like having good things to eat. For these things our soul—our core nature—ought to sing His praises, blessing Him as the One who is the Solution to any difficult situation we might face. All that is within us, bless His holy name! (See Verse 1.)

❧ *Day 334* ❧

"Bless the LORD, O my soul, and forget not all His benefits: who forgives all your iniquities, who heals all your diseases, who redeems your life from destruction, who crowns you with lovingkindness and tender mercies, who satisfies your mouth with good things, so that your youth is renewed like the eagle's."

Psalm 103:2-5

Youth renewed like the eagle's" continues a similar mental picture of a baby being weaned as it grows; but rather than growing older and thus getting weaker, we're told that our childlike vigor improves as we grow in Him. Job makes the statement: "My glory is fresh within me, and my bow is renewed in my hand." (Job 29:20) What this means is as we expend energy in the daily grind of life (work, family, relationships, etc.) the Lord actually *renews* (repairs) our strength, returning us to as we were when we were young—fountains of energy.

Gesenius states that *renewed* (Strong's #H2318) connotes "polishing a sword"—the "newness of a sharp, polished splendid sword." We don't become worn out and dull with use; we're refined and honed as we expend energy! Like Isaiah 40:31, *eagle* (Strong's #H5404) is rooted in "laceration" (their sharp talons) and reinforces the idea of a sharpened sword, a sharp-eyed hunter.

❧ *Day 335* ❧

"Heal me, O LORD, and I shall be healed; save me, and I shall be saved, for You are my praise."

Jeremiah 17:14

*T*he context of this verse is the LORD, through His mouthpiece Jeremiah, showing the distinction between the person who trusts in Him, and the person who trusts in false gods, or in the arm of flesh. God states that man's heart is deceitfully wicked, and He alone is qualified to judge it, rendering to the person what they deserve, good or bad, depending on the condition of their heart. (Verses 9-10)

Likewise, because mankind is inherently wicked, He alone is the only Being who can fix that condition, the perfect Surgeon who can replace a hardened heart with a soft heart that yearns to follow His perfect ways. (See Ezekiel 36:26; 1 Samuel 10:9.)

When we talk about shelter from the storms of life, and the role we play in that shelter by following after God wholeheartedly, we must also remember that it is His grace which is sufficient for us (2 Corinthians 12:9) and it is only His Spirit that can create the ability to yearn for His ways. (See Zechariah 4:6.) It all stems from Him.

✒ *Day 336* ✒

*"Heal me, O L*ORD*, and I shall be healed; save me, and I shall be saved, for You are my praise"*

Jeremiah 17:14

It takes the LORD's power, rooted in His mercy, to heal and to save. Our good intentions toward Him are not enough to provide shelter from the storm. It is completely instigated by Him, and all we can do is walk in that grace, allowing His Spirit to change our "desperately wicked" hearts. (Verse 9) The marginalia has that translated as "incurably sick."

"Who can know it?" is rhetorical; only *He* can know it. That word is *yada* (Strong's #H3045), which most properly means "ascertain: to perceive, discern, discriminate, distinguish, recognize." It speaks of "revealing" the inward intention of the heart. Since only He can ascertain the wickedness of the heart, only He is able to cure that which is "incurably sick."

Jeremiah understood this. It's as if he was saying, "If You heal me, I'll be healed. If You save me, I'll be saved." There's no other way. That's why He is our "praise." That word's (Strong's #H8416) root means "to boast," literally to "flash forth sound or color" and carries the connotation of "like a madman, a fool." Boast clamorously in His goodness!

❧ Day 337 ❦

"He has delivered us from the power of darkness and conveyed us into the kingdom of the Son of His love, in whom we have redemption through His blood, the forgiveness of sins."

Colossians 1:13-14

*D*eliverance in the Greek (Strong's #G4506) carries an association with "flowing," like the current of running water flows from one place to another. The idea expressed here is that God rushes to draw us to Him, like a river's current pushing us from one place (darkness) to another (Christ's kingdom.) We are rescued from drowning in darkness, taken to the high ground by His Son's blood. *Conveyed* (Strong's #G3179) also speaks of being carried away from one place to another, transferred into the kingdom of light from the kingdom of darkness. This entire passage creates a mental image of the God Himself rushing in like water and carrying us away into His presence through the flowing blood of Jesus Christ.

Jesus talks about these rivers of living water (John 7:38) flowing out of the bellies of those who believe in His ability to rescue them, redeeming them through His blood. What an overwhelming word picture—the Spirit as rushing Water, transplanting us into a new kingdom!

❧ *Day 338* ❧

"He has delivered us from the power of darkness and conveyed us into the kingdom of the Son of His love, in whom we have redemption through His blood, the forgiveness of sins."

Colossians 1:13-14

*P*ower (Strong's #G1849) in this passage speaks of authority or right, stemming from a root verb meaning "it is lawful (to do something.)" If we are not in the kingdom of Christ, we are under the authority of *darkness* (Strong's #G4655), which speaks of "ignorance, ungodliness and immorality." We are "obscured" (hidden in shade) from the light of Jesus. (See John 8:12.) There is no partway saved; it is either the one rule of darkness, or the one rule of the Son. Until we are transferred into the kingdom of heaven, darkness has a *right*, that means, the jurisdiction, to take mastery over us. It takes being swept away by the blood of our Lord to sever that authority.

"Son of His love" is important to note. The word used here is *agape*, meaning it is because of God the Father's great love for His Son that He extends the offer of deliverance to us. As God loves Jesus, He loves us, and if we honor His Son as He honors Him, we are assured the "forgiveness of sins." We are sons because Jesus is *the* Son. (See 1 John 3:1.)

☙ *Day 339* ❧

"For as the heavens are high above the earth, so great is His mercy toward those who fear Him; as far as the east is from the west, so far has He removed our transgressions from us."

Psalm 103:11-12

*H*is mercy is toward those who fear Him. God's love is unchanging toward each person who has ever lived on this planet, but His mercy is reserved for those who love Him in return. To love God is to fear (reverence and obey) Him. (See John 14:15.) For those who do, they will find an unending fountain of mercy. We outlined *mercy* (Strong's #H2617) previously as meaning "eager, ardent desire" to show kindness to a person, as a king who shows pity on a subject, inclining the head toward them in favor. This desire to be good, full of lovingkindness, toward those who fear Him is as high as the heavens are above the earth—that's very high!

Heavens (Strong's #H8064) is the plural of a singular word, meaning two different degrees of heaven: the atmosphere above the earth, the sky where the clouds move, and also outer space ("the ether") where the "celestial bodies revolve." Modern science holds this visible "heaven" to be infinite, expanding outward indefinitely. There's always more space, as there is always more mercy!

"For as the heavens are high above the earth, so great is His mercy toward those who fear Him; as far as the east is from the west, so far has He removed our transgressions from us."

Psalm 103:11-12

Likewise as outer space is infinite, showing God's mercy is never ending for those who fear Him, this passage also shows that our transgressions are removed from us to an unlimited degree. East to west is following the path of the sun, which is unchanging and unalterable. Since the moment the earth was created, it has followed the same trail around the sun on its set path in the cosmos. Just as assuredly as the sun will *never* set in the east and rise in the west, God separates us from our sins—the east will never meet the west.

That's why it's not north to south. If we walk in a straight-line north, we'll eventually reach "the south" till we end up where we started. But because of the earth's rotation, if we follow the sun walking in a straight-line west, it never becomes "east." Through our faith in Jesus, God has removed (the verb is in the present infinitive, continuous tense) our sins from us to an incalculable distance. You have found mercy and forgiveness to a countless, limitless degree!

⊰ Day 341 ⊱

"Repent therefore and be converted, that your sins may be blotted out, so that times of refreshing may come from the presence of the Lord…"

Acts 3:19

*R*epent and *convert* (Strong's #G3340, #G1994) have similar meanings in the Greek. Repentance is literally "changing your mind, turning back on the way you were thinking." True repentance is to turn around and go the other way—from the rebellious thoughts and actions toward God. That's why Hebrews 6:1 mentions both "repentance from dead works" *and* "faith toward God." It means to change your mind about sin and think like God thinks about it, in a heartfelt and sincere manner. It doesn't mean you won't ever fall short—it means you return back to God's way with a genuine and earnest mindset not to "turn around" again back toward sin.

Convert is a compound word, adding double strength to the idea of turning around to go toward God. It means to turn, and *really* turn, doubly emphatic. Both of these words speak of deliberate *movement,* turning oneself around and walking toward the Lord's presence. From that position the "times of refreshing" will come. Shelter from the storm is rooted in a genuine, forceful pursuit of God's presence *and* turning from sin.

⊰ Day 342 ⊱

"Repent therefore and be converted, that your sins may be blotted out, so that times of refreshing may come from the presence of the Lord…"

Acts 3:19

*B**lotted out* (Strong's #G1813) is another compound word, the root of which is "anoint, smear" added to the preposition for "out, away." It is not merely forgiveness of sins; it is the obliteration of sins. The word means to completely smear away, to wipe out, erase, "to wash away every part." The blood of Jesus not only provides a covering for sin (forgiveness), but an actual eradication of sin, as if it hadn't happened in the first place. God the Father cannot abide with sin, so it's not good enough to just "look past it"—it must be destroyed. That doesn't mean we are incapable of sinning while still on this earth; it means when we repent and convert, the Lord blots our sin away, smothering it out completely in His blood.

Times of refreshing is most properly "appointed seasons of cooling off," meaning resting and catching one's breath. The Latin word used here is *refrigerium*, which is where the word refrigerator comes from. The idea is God gives us periods of time in the midst of life's storms to chill out and refresh ourselves in His presence.

☙ Day 343 ❧

"And with great power the apostles gave witness to the resurrection of the Lord Jesus. And great grace was upon them all.

Acts 4:33

*T*his verse is the result of Verse 4:31: "And when they had prayed, the place where they were assembled together was shaken; and they were all filled with the Holy Spirit, and they spoke the word of God with boldness." One of the primary signs of being baptized in the Holy Spirit is speaking the word of God with *boldness*. The context of this rumbling encounter with His Spirit was the "threats" of the Gentiles against the early Christians (Verse 29), and the disciples' need for boldness to stand against those threats and deliver the word of God (that is, with healings, signs and wonders, see Verse 30.)

As important as one's heavenly prayer language is for those "times of refreshing," (see Isaiah 28:11-12)—of equal importance is the boldness that comes from God's Spirit, enabling the believer to have "great power" and "great grace" in the midst of adversity to see the supernatural acts of God transform the lives of those around them. When we speak of shelter from the storm, it's not just hiding ourselves in God from them, it's also boldly launching out with power and grace *through* them!

ᘏᑞᘏ *Day 344* ᘏᑞᘏ

"And with great power the apostles gave witness to the resurrection of the Lord Jesus. And great grace was upon them all.

Acts 4:33

*G*reat *power* and *great grace* (Strong's #G3173, #G1411, #G5485) is *megas* attached to *dynamis* (like the word dynamite) and *charis* (like the words charismatic and charity) respectively. Those are what gives "witness to the resurrection of the Lord Jesus." We use mega in English all the time to show an exceeding, superlative degree of whatever it's attached to. Like, megabucks or megavitamins. Compare Jesus referring to Himself as the *Alpha* and *Omega* (Revelation 22:13)—He is saying, "I AM the end all, be all, the first and the last, to the *mega* degree."

The infilling of the Holy Spirit produces mega amounts of power and grace within the life of the believer. Exceptional, supreme amounts of explosive acts of extreme charity—everything you need to get the job done: giving witness to Christ's resurrection in the name of signs, wonders, miracles, healings, you name it. We're not just called to cower in the back, waiting for the terrible storm to pass. Rather, we're called to go forth boldly and bring that mega-ness to the world at large!

❧ *Day 345* ❧

"And He said to her, 'Daughter, your faith has made you well. Go in peace, and be healed of your affliction.'"

Mark 5:34

*M*ade you well" (Strong's #G4982) can be rendered "has saved you." The root word is *sozo*, which you probably recognize as the word for "salvation," in all its many facets: spiritually, mentally, emotionally and physically. The salvation that Christ offers is complete. We often refer to the leper in Matthew 8. This man knew Jesus was capable of healing him, that's why he came and worshipped Him. (Verse 2) What he needed to know was if Jesus was *willing* to heal him—was He willing to touch his leprous flesh and regard him as equal and as worthy as the other people He had touched. We know Jesus' staunch, unwavering reply: "I am willing." (Verse 3)

I like to think, just as the leper in Matthew 8, this woman with the issue of blood needed more than just a physical healing, but complete *sozo*, a healing of the mental, emotional reproach because of her disease. With both people, it was their boldness to approach the Son of God in faith, disregarding the public's revulsion at their "uncleanness," which brought about their complete salvation. No matter what we face, we must have that same boldness and faith. He is willing—salvation is ours!

❧ *Day 346* ❧

"And He said to her, 'Daughter, your faith has made you well. Go in peace, and be healed of your affliction.'"

Mark 5:34

*H*ealed of your affliction" is translated "whole of thy plague" in the original King James. *Whole* (Strong's #G5199) is where we get the English word *hygienic.* It refers to soundness of body, healthy, hearty and hale. So it *is* referring to physical health; but in turn, *whole* comes from a base word (Strong's #G837) meaning "to grow up, enlarge, increase," or augment—compare the Greek to the word *auxiliary.* Faith makes us whole, in the most complete sense of the word. It makes us grow up, increase, augmented so that we can "go in peace" throughout our lives.

Further corroboration that faith yields peace and wholeness in spirit, soul and body—the word *affliction* (Strong's #G3148) is literally a whip or a scourge and figuratively is used for a plague, "calamity and misfortune." Most likely, it stems from a word meaning "to squeeze" and refers to chewing, eating, consuming, devouring—to gnaw. Compare to the English word *masticate.* Our faith in the Lord makes us whole of our plagues, that which scourges or gnaws on us. Thank the Lord for His salvation!

✢ *Day 347* ✤

"Now faith is the substance of things hoped for, the evidence of things not seen."

Hebrews 11:1

*F*aith is not hope. Biblically they are distinct, though faith springs from hope. They're both vitally important. If you have no hope, your faith will wither away. If you have no faith, you cannot keep hope alive. They're tied together, hand-in-hand. But it is faith that moves mountains, not hope. Faith is what activates that peace, wholeness and health we've been talking about the last couple days, not just hoping for it. The word *substance* (Strong's #G5287) is a compound word that literally translates "under-standing." Yes, that's like the word we use "understanding;" but in a concrete sense, the foundation of a building that "stands under" what is established, holding it up, undergirding and supporting the structure.

Faith is firm and set in place, upholding the construction of hope. It doesn't matter what faith doesn't see in the present—it remains fixed and determined till it *does* see what it hopes for. What faith hopes for is the manifestation of love (the God-kind of love, *agape*) in all its facets, which solves any problem faith faces. (See 1 Corinthians 13:13.)

✎ *Day 348* ✎

"Now faith is the substance of things hoped for, the evidence of things not seen."

Hebrews 11:1

*S*ubstance is the Greek word *hypostasis* (again, Strong's #G5287), which you'll probably recognize from the theological term "hypostatic union" of Christ—being both fully God and fully Man at the same time, in the same body. Hypostasis refers to the "underlying substance or essence, the fundamental reality that supports everything else." (Merriam-Webster's Dictionary) So, in Christ's case, His essence doesn't change: He is eternally divine, the One true God—everything else following is built on this. Concerning faith, it is the underlying substance, the essential, fundamental thing that everything following (that is, hope and love) is built on. Faith *is* a substance, a real, quantifiable "thing." It can be measured and gauged. (See Romans 12:3.)

Evidence (Strong's #G1650) is only used one other place in the New Testament, 2 Timothy 3:16, for "reproof." The idea conveyed here is faith "proves" or "tests" the conviction of hope. It is all that is needed to keep hope alive. Faith is in the present, hope is in the future, and love is the ultimate endgame of both. (Again, 1 Corinthians 13:13.)

❧ Day 349 ❧

"And when Jesus went out He saw a great multitude; and He was moved with compassion for them, and healed their sick."

Matthew 14:14

If faith is the bedrock for hope, then compassion is the bedrock for love. It is the motivating factor that unlocks God's mercy for the people. There cannot be agape love without the force of compassion driving it. Compassion is empathy and lovingkindness directed upon the needs of others. It is an act of selflessness. Our father, James Maloney, taught that compassion was *focused love*, a divine flow of love concentrated toward the needs of humanity that could be developed and nurtured just like hope and faith. It doesn't happen automatically in people's lives. A conscious effort must be made to follow after love, and from that pursuit springs the Spirit's gifts in action. (See 1 Corinthians 14:1.)

God's shelter from the storm is His focused love on us. It is rooted in His unchanging grace (remember, that's favor bestowed on the unworthy) and mercy. His compassion is a by-product of His existence. It's not something He has, it's something that He is. So pursuing love, and its foundation, compassion is simply pursuing Him.

167

⊷ *Day 350* ⊷

"And when Jesus went out He saw a great multitude; and He was moved with compassion for them, and healed their sick."

Matthew 14:14

You are probably aware that *compassion* in the Greek (Strong's #G4697) literally means to "have the bowels yearn." The Greeks thought that compassion originated in the intestines, because such deep feelings of love and sympathy for another could actually be felt in one's guts. Empathy is feeling as another feels, and here we see that the hurts of the multitude panged Jesus. He felt their pain, so to speak, and it moved Him to compassion, yielding that divine flow of love which ended with their healing. The gifts of the Spirit are tied to the manifestation, or expression, of love (that is, compassion.)

You've also probably heard that concept: if you're seeking something for yourself, go serve the needs of others, and you'll find what you're looking for. There is an awful lot of truth in that notion. Taking the focus off your needs (which are just as valid and needful as another's) doesn't simply "distract" you from your issues. Rather, following the divine flow of love has a reciprocal action. The gifts of the Spirit at the end of that love trail flow both ways, to the person in need and back to yourself.

✠ *Day 351* ✠

"Likewise the Spirit also helps in our weaknesses. For we do not know what we should pray for as we ought, but the Spirit Himself makes intercession for us with groanings which cannot be uttered. Now He who searches the hearts knows what the mind of the Spirit is, because He makes intercession for the saints according to the will of God."

Romans 8:26-27

Likewise connects this passage to Paul's earlier discourse. It's in the same vein as his previous inspired thoughts, which were on living according to the Spirit (life) or living according to the carnal mind (death.) It's a very heavy segment in Scripture: the law of the Spirit of life in Christ Jesus versus the law of sin and death. (Verse 2) It is that same Spirit (Verse 11), the one who gives life through Jesus, that *likewise* helps us overcome the weaknesses of the flesh tied to the law of sin and death.

The original King James translates "weaknesses" as *infirmities* (Strong's #G769) which is literally "without strength." The word can speak of weakness caused by illness or disease as well as feebleness and frailty of the soul: the inability to "do what's right" or understand a situation. The Spirit of life helps us with our infirmities, no matter where they come from.

❧ *Day 352* ❧

"Likewise the Spirit also helps in our weaknesses. For we do not know what we should pray for as we ought, but the Spirit Himself makes intercession for us with groanings which cannot be uttered. Now He who searches the hearts knows what the mind of the Spirit is, because He makes intercession for the saints according to the will of God."

Romans 8:26-27

Verse 28 speaks of "all things" working together for good. But it is tied into Verses 26-27 here: the Spirit making intercession for us, and those things working together for good because it is "according to the will of God." In other words, it takes the Spirit working through us to pray according to the will of God—it is *those things* that will work together for good.

God works according to His will, not our desires—those are the things that will come to pass "for good" because they originate within His mind. When we pray in the Spirit, we are praying according to His will, and then those things will work together for our good. The life of the Spirit is produced when we pray in the Spirit, and He helps us overcome our weaknesses, whatever they may be. That is the essence of shelter from the storm: the Spirit praying through us, for us!

☙ *Day 353* ❧

"Blessed is the man who walks not in the counsel of the ungodly, nor stands in the path of sinners, nor sits in the seat of the scornful; but his delight is in the law of the LORD, and in His law he meditates day and night. He shall be like a tree planted by the rivers of water, that brings forth its fruit in its season, whose leaf also shall not wither; and whatever he does shall prosper."

Psalm 1:1-3

Walk, stand, and sit covers any activity we might perform during the day. None of our activities are to be ungodly, sinful or scornful. Further, by night, we're to be meditating in the Word. So David takes care of pretty much every moment of our lives, declaring all our time is to be devoted to the law of the LORD. Now we live in the age of our Lord, Jesus, under His new covenant. The law of Christ (Galatians 6:2) is much more condensed than the Old Testament, fulfilling the entire Law of God with just two requirements. (See Matthew 22:37-40.)

Since love is the condition for completion of Christ's law (John 13:34-35), all of our walking, standing, sitting and sleeping is to be rooted in love, for our God and our fellow man. There can't be any shortcuts, all day, every day. The love walk is the key to unlocking all aspects of shelter from the storm!

⊰ *Day 354* ⊱

"Blessed is the man who walks not in the counsel of the ungodly, nor stands in the path of sinners, nor sits in the seat of the scornful; but his delight is in the law of the Lord, *and in His law he meditates day and night. He shall be like a tree planted by the rivers of water, that brings forth its fruit in its season, whose leaf also shall not wither; and whatever he does shall prosper."*

Psalm 1:1-3

*P*rosper (Strong's #H6743) is a verb that's translated by Gesenius to mean "to go over or through, like a river; to attack or fall upon, like the Spirit falls upon a man." The word means "to rush or push forward, to break out or advance." It's translated "come mightily" in another translation. (New American Standard Version, 2013, 1 Sam. 10:6) This fits well with the mental picture created by a "tree planted by rivers of water." The person who walks, stands, sits and sleeps "in His law" will be like this type of strong tree, fed by the water of the Spirit.

Prosperity, then, is a state of being, a condition of existence that is rooted in our pursuit of fulfilling the law of Christ through love. Similar to the Hebraic concept of peace, which is succinctly encapsulated in the notion of "having a prosperous journey through life," prosperity is a result of walking consistently with Him.

❧ *Day 355* ❧

"God is not a man, that He should lie, nor a son of man, that He should repent. Has He said, and will He not do? Or has He spoken, and will He not make it good?"

Numbers 23:19

We discussed before that it is only the purposes of God which will be prosperous. "For I am God, and there is no other; I am God, and there is none like Me, declaring the end from the beginning, and from ancient times things that are not yet done, saying, 'My counsel shall stand, and I will do all My pleasure…'" (Isaiah 46:9-10) Only that which is lined up with His counsel will stand, which is why it's so important to have the Spirit making intercession for us—so that we are praying according to the will of God.

Prosperity, as the Bible defines it, is the purposes of God being completed in our lives. As we walk out the law of Christ, that divine flow of love for our God and for our fellow humans, we can be assured we're smack dab in the middle of God's will, so that His favor is flowing through us toward others and, in turn, reciprocating back into our lives. All of these keys we've been discussing, faith, hope, love, etc., go hand in hand with each other. The purpose of this life is to develop those attributes that unlock the "true riches" (Luke 16:11) of Christian life.

"God is not a man, that He should lie, nor a son of man, that He should repent. Has He said, and will He not do? Or has He spoken, and will He not make it good?"

Numbers 23:19

We trust in God's mercy, His grace, His lovingkindness and favor. We also need to trust in His trustworthiness. Remember, we're not dealing with a human being here. We're dealing with the divine Being, the only One, the perfect One. It's peculiar how many Christians trust God for their ultimate salvation, and yet don't take Him at His Word concerning all the other benefits (Psalm 103:2) of following Him. The physical healing, daily provisions, peace and joy in *this* life, are often left up to some nebulous, "if it be Thy will" mentality.

But God isn't a man. He isn't made of the same "stuff" as we are. His substance and existence are completely "other" than what we're made of. "For My thoughts are not your thoughts, nor are your ways My ways…" (Isaiah 55:8) That same statement continues with, "So shall My word be that goes forth from My mouth; it shall not return to Me void, but it shall accomplish what I please, and it shall prosper in the thing for which I sent it." (Verse 11) We can trust Him to do what He says He will do in His Word. All of it.

❧ *Day 357* ❧

"...For I am God, and there is no other; I am God, and there is none like Me, declaring the end from the beginning, and from ancient times things that are not yet done, saying, 'My counsel shall stand, and I will do all My pleasure...'"

Isaiah 46:9-10

*T*his passage is worth spending a bit more time with. When we talk about God, the only One, who is completely "other" than us, and therefore, trustworthy because He isn't subjected to the same failures that humanity is plagued with—the concept of God's singleness of existence must also incorporate His eternality. The primary reason why God is trustworthy is because He has *already* set His counsel on every moment of our lives *before* they ever happened. Nothing is a surprise to Him, no trial you'll face, just as no success you'll ever achieve.

God is *working backward*, at least to our limited ability to understand "eternity." I suppose technically speaking He is working in the ever-present "now"—there isn't a past, present or future to Him. It's all just "now." But this passage makes it clear He's declared the end before it ever began. Because of His place as being above all, in all, through all (Ephesians 4:6), at the same moment in time and space—we can trust Him to do as He says!

"...For I am God, and there is no other; I am God, and there is none like Me, declaring the end from the beginning, and from ancient times things that are not yet done, saying, 'My counsel shall stand, and I will do all My pleasure...'"

Isaiah 46:9-10

Now, just because God is existing through the past, present and future simultaneously, knowing all and plotting all His pleasure from "ancient times things that are not yet done," *we* as finite beings on this earth do not have that state of understanding. So, this all swings back around to *trust*. Just as we trust Jesus to save us in future eternity, we must also learn to trust He *is* saving us in the present. It's wonderful to have that assurance about our future, that's the most important thing, of course. But the purpose of this devotional has been to show that shelter is provided for the storms of *this* life. We'll have no storms in eternity, and books like this won't be necessary.

In the meantime, it's super important that we develop trust in God's otherness, alongside His mercy and grace, love and power, to know that He will "perfect that which concerns" us (Psalm 138:8) because He has already finished what He intends to do for you and through you before there ever was a *you*!

❧ *Day 359* ❧

"For a righteous man may fall seven times and rise again, but the wicked shall fall by calamity."

Proverbs 24:16

The context of this verse is "do not be envious of evil men…" (Verse 1) This passage is a magnificent discourse comparing the actions of the wise to the actions of the foolish, which is called "evil" and "sin." (Verses 8,9) We're admonished to "deliver those drawn toward death, and hold back those stumbling to the slaughter" (Verse 11) while not desiring to "be with them." (Again, Verse 1.) Part of walking in love is being our brother's keeper, but not falling into the same traps (calamities) that they do. Jesus taught the distinction between sheep and goats, the wise and the foolish. (See Matthew 25:31-46.) It takes wisdom not to fall into troubles.

That doesn't mean you won't fall. Wisdom isn't a "holier than thou" virtue. In fact, that's pretty much the *opposite* of wisdom. But when you stumble, if you're wise, you'll learn from those trips, get up, and build your house on wisdom and understanding. (Verse 3) Proverbs 4:6-7 tells us to "get wisdom." That means it's a process, working toward the goal of becoming a wise person, as opposed to a foolish person. And this passage of scripture outlines some powerful steps toward that goal.

❧ Day 360 ❧

"For a righteous man may fall seven times and rise again, but the wicked shall fall by calamity."

Proverbs 24:16

*S*even (Strong's #H7651) here is the number 7, but we know that in biblical numerology, it signifies "completion" or "fullness" because the word for "seven" has the same consonants as the word for "complete, full." It comes from a root meaning "to swear an oath." The idea conveyed here is that someone would swear seven times to show they *really* meant it; they called it "to seven oneself." People would bind themselves by seven things because the number was sacred—as in, on the seventh day, God rested, or completed His work. (See Genesis 21:28.)

The point here, in this verse, is to show the wise person's dedication to "getting wisdom." Going on to perfection, completion and binding themselves to that noble endeavor. *Calamity* (Strong's #H7451) on the other hand, is translated "mischief" in the King James and comes from a root meaning "evil, bad" in its many facets: "distress, misery, injury, hurt," Those who are foolish, who don't bind themselves to the godly pursuit of "righteousness," are bound, instead, to fall into the pit of calamity, from which they are unable to "rise again." Seek shelter, seek wisdom, seven yourself to it!

❧ Day 361 ❧

"For the eyes of the LORD run to and fro throughout the whole earth, to show Himself strong on behalf of those whose heart is loyal to Him."

2 Chronicles 16:9

People who think that God is uninterested in their daily lives are mistaken according to this verse. Often their feelings of being "on their own" when dealing with life's difficulties are because of their reliance upon another source, rather than relying upon God to carry them through the circumstances. With their own strength and intelligence, or by relying upon others' strength and intelligence, they may be able to get out of the problem eventually; but often it's a partial, temporary solution, or not the best-case scenario.

The context of this verse is really a reproof that God sent to Asa, king of Judah. The king of Israel had started construction on a town with the intent of harassing Judah. Instead of relying upon God, as he had done with previous conflicts, Asa relied upon his alliance with the king of Syria, who invaded Israel so that construction of the city had to be abandoned. Asa fixed his immediate problem, but he missed the bigger picture: the opportunity to subdue Syria. Our reliance must be on God alone for the best outcomes. Don't be like Asa.

❧ *Day 362* ❦

"For the eyes of the LORD run to and fro throughout the whole earth, to show Himself strong on behalf of those whose heart is loyal to Him."

2 Chronicles 16:9

*A*nd it wasn't as if Asa had out-and-out sinned by relying on the king of Syria, but God told him he'd acted foolishly, nevertheless. 1 Kings 15:11 shows Asa doing what's right in the sight of the LORD, but incompletely. He removed *some* of the idolatry from the land, but he permitted the places of idol worship to remain.

If Asa had sought God's counsel on how to deal with the king of Israel, it would have turned out a complete victory—routing not only Israel, but Syria too. God is *looking* for opportunities to show His strength, but what He's really looking for is loyalty to Him and Him alone. *Loyal* (Strong's #H8003) means "whole, complete, perfect." The word speaks of a covenant of peace between Him and His people. As they kept their end of the agreement, it enabled Him to "show Himself strong" on their behalf. People who are wholly, completely, perfectly committed to His ways. It isn't so much that their *actions* are always perfect, but their *hearts* are 100% committed to Him always. (See 1 Samuel 13:14; Acts 13:22.)

✢ *Day 363* ✢

"The Lord upholds all who fall, and raises up all who are bowed down. The eyes of all look expectantly to You, and You give them their food in due season. You open Your hand and satisfy the desire of every living thing."

Psalm 145:14-16

While the eyes of the Lord run to and fro, looking for hearts solely committed to Him, *our* eyes, as His children, are to "look expectantly" to Him to meet our needs, to "satisfy the desire." Psalm 34:7 tells us, "Delight yourself also in the Lord, and He shall give you the desires of your heart." Now, it's true that desire does mean "the things we want," but we need to remind ourselves that ultimately *He* is the desire. The conditional clause to Psalm 34:7 is delighting ourselves in *Him*.

When He is our delight, our sole desire, it unlocks an extremely special state of being, a relationship with Him that releases His strength and wisdom in every situation. It isn't that He's playing favorites—this conditional state of existence is available to all. And it isn't that He's changed or moved in the slightest—this state was *always* available. Only, *we* are the ones who've come into alignment with Him. We need to discipline our lives to enter into this kind of wonderful reality wherein we are "upheld" and "raised" up in every circumstance.

✺᛫ Day 364 ᛫✺

"The Lᴏʀᴅ upholds all who fall, and raises up all who are bowed down. The eyes of all look expectantly to You, and You give them their food in due season. You open Your hand and satisfy the desire of every living thing."

Psalm 145:14-16

*D*esire (Strong's #H7522) is often translated "delight" or "favor." The word stems from a root meaning "to be pleased with, to accept favorably." It's the ever-present goodwill of God directed toward "every living thing." Rather, as we see in Luke 2:14, it is the people in "whom He is well-pleased." (American Standard Version Bible, 1929, Luke 2:14) That is, those who "look expectantly" to Him, whose "heart is loyal to Him." As with all biblical promises, this satisfaction of desire is conditional. Since God does not move and does not change (Malachi 3:6), *we* must move, *we* must change.

"Due season" (Strong's #H6256) is the cognate of the Greek word *kairos*, which we've looked at previously. Both words are speaking of an appointed time, a specially created moment that God foreordained to happen as a season within the regular flow of calendar time. We've all heard the phrase, "God is never late, and He's never early." We learn patience and dependence on our Lord while waiting for that "due season," but it will come!

❧ Day 365 ❦

"He heals the brokenhearted and binds up their wounds. He counts the number of the stars; He calls them all by name. Great is our LORD, and mighty in power; His understanding is infinite. The LORD lifts up the humble; He casts the wicked down to the ground."

Psalm 147:3-6

*B*rokenhearted (Strong's #H7665) is a stronger word in the Hebrew than what we think of when we say "heartbroken." It means "maimed, crippled, wrecked, crushed, ruptured, smashed, shattered, burst." A spirit broken into pieces. The word is used when speaking of literal shipwrecks. The word *heals* (Strong's #H7495) as you probably know is *rapha*, the covenant name of Jehovah the Healer. (Exodus 15:26) It means "heal by stitching." So, our Lord stitches up the crushed and smashed soul.

He binds the *wounds* (Strong's #H6094)—which is literally "sorrows." Of interest, this word also means "an idol," properly something that's carved. This speaks of "vexations, grievances" that come from worshiping something (anything) other than God. He binds (as in to chain up) those vexations, not permitting them to affect His people once they turn to Him wholeheartedly. This verse goes way beyond just healing a broken heart!

183

❧ *Day 366* ❧

"He heals the brokenhearted and binds up their wounds. He counts the number of the stars; He calls them all by name. Great is our LORD, and mighty in power; His understanding is infinite. The LORD lifts up the humble; He casts the wicked down to the ground."

Psalm 147:3-6

*G*reat is our Lord's power and understanding, infinitely so. It's such that He calls each star by its name. That should bring great comfort to you and me. If He counts the stars, He's certainly capable of healing and binding our broken hearts and wounds. We serve an immeasurably powerful God! If there's any one thing this book is trying to convey: God is worthy of our worship. All of the "shelter from the storm" we've been outlining in this devotional is simply a consequence of serving Him without reservation.

The prime posture that God is looking for is *humility*. Approach the Lord from a stance of simplicity and sincerity, be honest and unpretentious, and He *will* lift you up. This is one of the greatest promises in all of scripture: "Humble yourselves in the sight of the Lord, and He will lift you up." (James 4:10) Everything you're in need of can be found in Him, and He longs to raise you up to ever-increasing heights in your relationship with Him!

Printed in the United States
by Baker & Taylor Publisher Services